SOUTHEAST ASIAN REGIONALISM
NEW ZEALAND PERSPECTIVES

SOUTHEAST ASIAN REGIONALISM
NEW ZEALAND PERSPECTIVES

NICHOLAS TARLING

LSEAS

INSTITUTE OF SOUTHEAST ASIAN STUDIES
SINGAPORE

First published in Singapore in 2011 by ISEAS Publishing
Institute of Southeast Asian Studies
30 Heng Mui Keng Terrace
Pasir Panjang
Singapore 119614

E-mail: publish@iseas.edu.sg
Website: http://bookshop.iseas.edu.sg

A limited amount of this book appeared in Nicholas Tarling, *Regionalism in
Southeast Asia: To Foster the Political Will* (Abingdon: Routledge, 2006)

*The responsibility for facts and opinions in this publication rests exclusively
with the author and his interpretations do not necessarily reflect the views
or the policy of the publisher or its supporters.*

ISEAS Library Cataloguing-in-Publication Data

Tarling, Nicholas.
    Southeast Asian regionalism : New Zealand perspectives.
    1.   Southeast Asia—History—1945-
    2.   Regionalism—Southeast Asia—History.
    3.   Southeast Asia--Foreign relations.
    I.   Title.
DS526.7 T182   2011

ISBN 978-981-4311-49-6 (soft cover)
ISBN 978-981-4311-01-4 (E-book PDF)

Typeset by International Typesetters Pte Ltd
Printed in Singapore by Markono Print Media Pte Ltd

Contents

Southeast Asian Regionalism: New Zealand Perspectives

Nicholas Tarling

Introduction

With the disappearance of the imperial structures that had dominated Southeast Asia, newly-independent states had to develop foreign policies of their own. So far few of those states, if any, have been willing to allow the public to explore the documentary evidence of their activities that has no doubt been preserved. Somewhat paradoxically, historians must turn to the archives of external powers, which have largely adopted a thirty-year rule, though, as Chandran Jeshurun has said, it is "clearly untenable" to cite foreign diplomatic reports as "unquestionable proof of what actually transpired".[1] The diplomats of external powers were indeed often keenly interested in collecting information from ministers, in the office or at parties or on the golf course or otherwise, and from officials who might, for whatever purpose, convey or leak it more or less straightforwardly. In my recent book, *Regionalism in Southeast Asia* (Routledge, 2006), I was able to incorporate material from UK records on the development of the Southeast Asia Friendship and Economic Treaty (SEAFET), Association of Southeast Asia States (ASA), and Association of Southeast Asian Nations (ASEAN). The New Zealand archives contain not only reports from New Zealand diplomats but also from Australian and Canadian diplomats as well. The purpose of the present volume is to take account of this material without unduly duplicating the relevant chapters of the book.

In the earlier book I made the obvious but not always stated point that the new states of Southeast Asia were, though equal in sovereignty, unequal in power. That feature, of course, they shared with the rest of the world of states. Their geography and their history suggested, however, that it would be only too tempting to try to redress such imbalances by recourse to larger powers outside the region. That, it was also clear, was not likely to be readily accepted by the largest state in the region, Indonesia, which was bound to claim to be rather more than equal. In the longer term the states were able to handle the issue by at once asserting their independence, sovereignty and integrity, and at the same time forming a regional association on that very basis. The goal was only reached by a rather indirect route, and observers, and perhaps participants, were often pessimistic, mistaken, or even dismissive. The material from external archives nevertheless helps us to chart the route.

From SEAFET to ASA

It is striking that Malaya played so large a role in the many initiatives that marked the early phase, but perhaps not surprising. It had become independent of Britain in 1957, and though the two powers made an Anglo-Malayan defence agreement, it now had to ensure its security. Perhaps my previous book exaggerates the extent to which it formulated its policy in the light of its relationship with Indonesia. But it seems clear that, of all the relationships it had now to develop, one was crucial, even if it was not always best to say so. Indonesia was not only wrapped around Malaysia; it had armed itself to deal with domestic revolts and was challenging the former colonial power for West Irian (Papua).

No longer in the hands of a minor European state, the Indies were in the hands of a Republic, the most populous state in the region, proud of its record in winning independence and conscious of a leadership entitlement in international affairs, expressed, for example, in its role in the Afro-Asian movement since the Bandung conference of 1955. By not joining the U.S.-led SEATO (South East Asia Treaty Organisation) Malaya would avoid challenging Indonesia as well as China, and it did not want merely to rely on its defence agreement with the United Kingdom. Nor, however, did it want a merely bilateral engagement with Indonesia, which would imply another kind of dependence. Its regional initiatives sought an answer to the conundrum.

Early in February 1958, as the earlier book recounts, the Prime Minister, Tunku Abdul Rahman, visited Colombo and there urged closer cooperation among the smaller Southeast Asian countries. Southeast Asian countries, he said at a press conference on his return, were "too much inclined to dance to the tune of bigger nations. They should not concern themselves unduly with the world and Afro-Asian politics when they had problems of their own nearer at hand. An effort should be made to build up their own unity and understanding. If they did not do this, they would have to look outside the area for protection and the full meaning of independence would be lost."[2]

The Tunku, it was reported in Jakarta, had "a Southeast Asia cultural and economic alliance" in mind. "As part of the arrangement, or perhaps in lieu of it, there would be a drawing together of the Filipino, Indonesian and Malay peoples around a nucleus provided by the Federation." The Canadian Embassy in Indonesia thought he was flying a kite, but found that the Malayan Ambassador (Senu) had been instructed "to attempt to persuade the Indonesians of the desirability of some such arrangement.... their participation was essential because ... the possible growth of Communism in Indonesia and the threat to Malaya therefrom, was one of the principal considerations behind the whole idea." The Jakarta press had been critical, and the Canadians thought the proposal had little chance of acceptance. "Indonesia is almost certainly unready to sacrifice what she considers to be her position of influence among the larger group of Bandung powers for any formal alliance, Pan-Malayan, Southeast Asian or otherwise.... Indeed the Indonesians may well resent the suggestion that they accept leadership from Malaya, a nation they regard as their junior in age, experience and influence."[3]

The Canadian High Commission in Kuala Lumpur explored the idea of "a South-East Asia Club" with Zaiton Ibrahim bin Ahmad, then Principal Assistant Secretary at the Ministry of External Affairs (MEA). He put the emphasis on economic cooperation and cultural exchange. The initial core would be Malaya, the Philippines, and Indonesia, "in a good position to help each other because of their affinities of race and language". Indonesia might join even though the underlying aim was to "strengthen the countries' powers to resist Communism", since its leaders were really anti-communist, though they could not say so. Thailand, Zaiton thought, might be "the most logical first addition".[4]

Subandrio, the Indonesian Foreign Minister, made it clear that his government preferred bilateral agreements.[5] The Canadians explored the reasons for the negative reaction with Anwar Sani, Deputy Director of Asian and Pacific Affairs at the Ministry of Foreign Affairs (MFA). "Malaya and more especially the Philippines were, he said, too much under foreign influence to sponsor such a pact.... It would be desirable in Indonesia's view for the sponsors to recover their 'national identities' before striking out too far internationally."[6]

Asked by the Canadian High Commissioner (Heasman), the New Zealand Department of External Affairs found it difficult to comment on the Tunku's proposals: they changed in form on almost every occasion he put them forward. "This continuing imprecision suggests that the Malayan initiative is in large measure a reflection of a vague, but perceptible desire in some of the smaller countries of the South East Asian area — a desire for a form of cooperative association which they can feel is their own." They were "groping towards a purely South East Asian grouping, which would at once enhance the sense of unity of the area and keep them out of the quarrels of the major powers. At the same time, none of them would be prepared to give up the present substantial Western economic aid they now receive." The Malayan proposals faced the basic difficulty of "giving a sufficiently independent basis to the new grouping to attract Indonesia and others while still retaining the economic and political support and assistance of the West". Long-term, the development the Tunku envisaged could be in the Western interest. "It could encourage a sense of interdependence among South East Asian countries, with a consequent increase in their solidity against the Communist threat to the area as a whole. And, by introducing a regional basis of common interest among Asian countries, it might also do something to reduce the absorption of the Afro/Asian group with the racial antipathies which at present dominate and unify its activities."

It was difficult, the department concluded, to see any basis for economic cooperation among the countries. "To all of them trade with other countries is much more important than an expanded intraregional trade would be; they are largely competitors in the world market as producers of raw materials; and they must all rely, in varying degree, on capital investment from countries outside the area."[7]

In Singapore the Acting Commissioner for New Zealand, R.A. Lochore, found that British officials tended to think that the Tunku was mainly influenced by the forthcoming elections. Lochore himself thought it was more than a matter of electoral opportunism. The Tunku was "constantly aware that anything done for its own sake" — an investment charter, a federation of trade unions, a football federation — would "help to build up the autonomy of countries of South East Asia" and thus be "tacitly anti-Communist in effect". Probably, like other Southeast Asian leaders, he also saw the problem as "fundamentally one of containing Chinese influence in the area", whether it came from Peking or Taipei. What the Tunku now called SEAFET (South East Asia Friendship and Economic Treaty) might find little to do in the near future, but New Zealand's attitude should be "exploratory and approbatory". Lochore did not at all agree with the views of the Commonwealth Relations Office (CRO). "The obvious beginning is with the three countries of Malay stock, and the organization should not be launched at all except with the active support (and preferably leadership) of Indonesia."[8]

Lochore was alluding to the views developed in London by an interdepartmental meeting (Foreign Office, Commonwealth Relations Office, Board of Trade), which, as my earlier book recounted, had commended the idea of closer association, "a solution to the political problems of the area which in general we favour", but questioned the Tunku's tactics. The departments thought he should turn his attention northward. "Ideally we would like to see Burma, Thailand, Laos, Cambodia and South Vietnam included." Thailand was essential if the association were to have "any geographical cohesion", but, a prominent member of SEATO, it should not play too dominant a role at first.[9]

The New Zealand High Commission in Kuala Lumpur thought that the Tunku might have been "thinking on his feet" in Manila, "and attempting to forestall any attempt to persuade the Malayan Government to join SEATO".

Zaiton said the ministry was drawing up draft proposals that might be sent to the Philippines Government and followed by a second conference. The membership should be confined to Southeast Asia, "a recognizable geographic entity". Indonesia had not yet been given an outline of the proposals, but Zaiton acknowledged that it was "the next and most logical member of the grouping envisaged by the Tunku". Officials in Kuala Lumpur, the High Commission concluded, were "by no means certain that anything positive will emerge. Their present tendency is to play the thing quietly, determine their own views, find out to what extent these views accord with those of the Philippines and then, and only then, consider approaching the wider group of South East Asian countries."[10]

"The Tunku's plan is now passing through a period of consolidation and elaboration", Arthur Menzies of the Canadian High Commission reported. The founding members of SEAFET were to be Malaya and the Philippines. They would have liked to bring Indonesia in, but the chances of doing so did not on balance seem "robust". The Philippines' membership of SEATO must prejudice SEAFET in Indonesian eyes. "Our Embassy in Jakarta has reported that Indonesians fear that SEAFET membership would reduce their influence in other parts of the Afro-Asian world and would commit Indonesia to anti-Communism to an unwelcome degree." The fact that their "junior" Malaya put it forward also prejudiced SEAFET in Indonesians' eyes. Indonesia, on the other hand, was seeking to establish closer bilateral ties with Malaya, trying to sell a more comprehensive treaty than the Federation wanted to accept. "The apparent contradiction within the

Malayan and Indonesian attitudes presumably lies in a Malayan belief in the safety of numbers and Indonesian dislike of SEATO." Beyond the "inner circle", Thailand was the most likely candidate for membership. SEAFET could be quickly forgotten after the elections. But there seemed to be behind it "a genuine urge for increased cooperation and mutual knowledge among Southeast Asian nations who have been largely screened off from each other by western influence and control. This impulse is allied to a genuine wish for collaboration to help the small nations of this area to stand more firmly on their own feet and to be less economically and culturally dependent on the West."[11]

Now New Zealand High Commissioner in Ottawa, Foss Shanahan offered observations on the Malayan proposals based on his previous experience in Southeast Asia. The Tunku had, for example, mentioned the idea to him during a break in the meetings of the working party on the United Kingdom–Malaya Defence Agreement. "He did not then spell out the reasons which prompted him to suggest such an idea, but I think they are to be found, to some extent, in the conditions which exist in Malaya and South East Asia generally." In Malaya Indian opinion tended to be neutralist, and the Chinese were bound to be influenced by Peking. While he had "a strong feeling of affinity" with the United Kingdom and welcomed the Defence Agreement, "he is anxious to create another area of balance or strength within the region of South East Asia itself". He told Shanahan that all the countries of Southeast Asia were small and "would be noticed and effective only if they found some way of getting together". The

"Colombo Powers" — India, Pakistan, Sri Lanka, Burma, and Indonesia — was not an adequate regional grouping, and the Afro-Asian group was too concerned with North and Central Africa.

Economic cooperation had been "sporadic", and the post-colonial countries had "not yet developed the habit or attitude of mind which would suggest that they give a special priority to the question of their relations with their immediate neighbours". The Philippines was, however, anxious to demonstrate its independence of the United States, and it seemed that Malaya would go ahead with a treaty, though a two-power treaty would be "rather unfortunate because it would probably make it more difficult to widen its scope to include countries such as Burma, Thailand, Vietnam and Indonesia".

Though it should not, at least at that stage, be directly involved, New Zealand should encourage a wider grouping. The partners, as in most other treaties, would have "a variety of motives". In the Tunku's mind one of the values of a treaty and the cooperation it should promote was "greater political understanding which may lead to some affirmation of a general position on the question of the regional security of its members". The Indonesians might be reluctant to join, given reasons of prestige, "and the feeling that they have a role to play not just regionally but essentially on the world's stage". But New Zealand should do what it could to encourage them to take a favourable attitude towards joining, because it might "assist the process of creating stability in Indonesia and bring her into closer relations with the Countries of South East Asia".[12]

Felixberto Serrano, the Philippines Foreign Minister, visited Kuala Lumpur on his way to attend the SEATO conference in Wellington. On SEAFET he was "hopeful but vague". It would at first be bilateral, then Malaya and the Philippines would consider bringing others in.[13] Razak and Ismail, the Malayan leaders, found the Thai leaders enthusiastic when they visited Bangkok in June, Zaiton said, and they had undertaken to put some comments on Malaya's draft proposals in writing.[14] Foreign Minister Thanat subsequently visited other mainland capitals. Only two of the communiqués — those in Rangoon and Saigon — mentioned regional cooperation, the New Zealand Chargé in Bangkok (Charles Craw) noticed. Thanat said it would be "fatal to force the pace.... Cooperation had to come naturally in response to the genuine feelings of the countries concerned and if the proposals were quietly discussed he thought that progress would eventually be made. When asked whether in view of Indonesia's attitude he thought the scheme should be confined to the peninsular countries plus the Philippines, Thanat said that he believed that eventually Indonesia also might be interested."[15]

By November Malayan tactics had changed, as the British documents used in my previous book made clear. Ismail said that the Tunku had written to the Prime Ministers in Vietnam, Laos, Cambodia, Thailand, Burma, the Philippines, and Indonesia.[16] There had been a danger, a diplomat at the British High Commission commented, that the agreement might look too restrictive. That was probably why the Federation had dropped the original idea of a bilateral agreement with the Philippines, to which others could accede, in favour of a simultaneous approach.

Ghazali bin Shafie, then Deputy Permanent Secretary at the MEA, "was also hopeful — I think unduly so — that Indonesia might veer round."[17]

The following month, however, Prince Sihanouk made it clear that Cambodia could not join, lest it forsook neutrality. Thailand and the Philippines were both in SEATO, and only one part of Vietnam, the south, had been invited.[18] By March 1960 it was clear that the SEAFET proposal was, in the words of J.C. Crombie at the CRO in London, "doing very poorly". Indonesia had reportedly formally rejected the idea. Burma's reply was "disappointing", and Laos had not replied at all. The Philippines and Thailand were "apparently in favour", though the Thais stressed the need for more preparatory work. Visiting Kuala Lumpur in February (15–19 February 1960), President Ngo Dinh Diem had said the same.[19]

"The Burmese favour closer contacts between Southeast Asian countries but feel that the time is not yet ripe for a multilateral treaty", the Canadians understood. "They are also concerned, no doubt, to conclude their border settlement with Communist China without raising any issues which might antagonize their big Communist neighbour." The Soviet Ambassador in Rangoon told Arthur Menzies that his government approved Burma's attitude. "Even if SEAFET started out with economic and cultural co-operation goals it would inevitably become an extension of SEATO."[20]

In the event the Tunku decided to go ahead with SEAFET on the basis of membership by Malaya, the Philippines, and Thailand alone. A start had to be made somewhere, he said; an organization in being might be

I

more attractive than a mere plan.[21] The new association, he announced in July, would be called ASAS, Association of South East Asian States, not SEAFET. It might be more practicable, he said, to have multilateral agreements on particular projects than a treaty, and officials from Malaya, the Philippines, and Thailand would draw up a list. ASAS would explore the possibilities of regional cooperation in aviation, shipping, marketing and pricing primary products, and technical and administrative training and research.[22]

The decision to abandon a formal treaty seemed in Wellington to be "realistic and practical". If SEAFET had been carried through, it would have been an association of nations with close links with the West. "If regional co-operation is to be expanded on a broad and meaningful basis, it is important that uncommitted countries like Indonesia and Burma agree to participate. There seems a better prospect of this being achieved under the new more informal working relationship."[23] The Economic Division (B.M. Brown) was more cautious. "The whole trend towards regionalism is one of which New Zealand has cause to be wary, in Asia as well as Europe." Wherever possible, it should "stress that the interests of outside countries should not be neglected".[24]

Garcia visited Kuala Lumpur on 8–11 February, and Thanat followed on the 11th, for talks on ASAS with the Tunku and Serrano. In a communiqué issued on the 13th, the parties announced that they would set up an organization, starting with a working party.[25] The New Zealand High Commission had the impression that the Filipinos had been seeking to establish "a political and economic association, with something of an ideological basis". The Tunku, "conscious … that any organization which conveyed a too obvious anti-Communist character would be anathema to countries such as Indonesia and Burma", stressed economic aspects. Both Serrano and the Tunku expressed regret at Indonesia's "aloofness".[26]

In April, in the course of an interview with members of a Malayan study tour group in Jakarta, Subandrio described ASAS as "without substance" and "useless". For the time being there was no need for the formation of such an organization, "especially as the backgrounds of these states differ from each other. There must be bilateral relations first". The *Malay Mail* attacked his remarks editorially. The most popular explanation for Indonesia's attitude, it said, was that having pioneered the formation of the Afro-Asian bloc, it did not wish to join a more restricted group. "Moreover, it was believed that Indonesia felt herself to be the 'big brother' of the South-East Asian nations and considered that any alliance involving them should have her at its head. Instead, in the case of ASAS, Indonesia would be expected to join after others had achieved the credit of sponsoring the organization." If true, that was petty, it said, the New Zealand report adding that it was an interpretation that also had "considerable private support among Malayan officials".[27]

The first meeting of the Thai, Malayan, and Philippine working groups was scheduled for Bangkok in mid-June 1961. The communiqué issued on 22 June 1961 reiterated that the cooperation would be "non-political in character, independent in every way of any power bloc, and essentially one of joint endeavour in the economic and cultural fields". The conference had covered a wide range of possible forms of cooperation, discussed the organization of the association, and prepared a draft agenda for a meeting of foreign ministers. No details had been revealed, and the British Embassy remained doubtful that Thailand would "match the enthusiasm of the other two countries".[28]

The New Zealand High Commission in Kuala Lumpur discussed the meeting with one of the Malayan delegates. Welcoming the delegation, the Deputy Prime Minister of Thailand had made a speech with some unfortunate political overtones, "saying something to the effect that since SEATO was no longer prepared to do anything about Laos, it might well be a suitable field for the attention of the proposed new organization". Much concerned that this "raised the ghost of the original Philippines conception of the agreement as an Asian anti-Communist front", the Malayans sought clarification. The Deputy Prime Minister was mistaken, misreported, Sarit said. The meeting focused on economic matters, where the Malayans were more modest and better prepared than the Filipinos.[29]

The New Zealand Embassy in Bangkok could secure no comments from the Thai officials, but made some comments of its own. "The Thais could hardly afford to turn their backs on ASAS and therefore have played along with it." The government thought it could make "quite effective use of any trend towards Southeast Asian 'togetherness' by emphasizing that if its Western allies (having let down Laos) are not as concerned as they should be about Thailand then the Thais must redouble their efforts to look after themselves and at the same time seek friends among their neighbours". Indeed Thanat had made the point on 19 July when speaking to the American Association. Laos, he said, was a springboard for aggrandizement, but, without oil, uranium, or investments, it offered no incentive for the West to defend it. Thailand had to re-examine its position and cultivate its neighbours. Obviously he did not expect that ASAS could do much to save his country from the Communists. "Indeed he did not mention ASAS at all, no doubt deliberately, in order to leave the impression that Thailand might go a great deal further and eventually adopt neutralism of the Burmese and Cambodian type." Chargé Craw did not think that expressions of disappointment at the Western attitude on Laos could be dismissed as blackmail. Thanat was "quite sincere in his efforts to arouse his own people and Thailand's neighbours to the dangers which face them.... He would undoubtedly like to see a widespread Southeast Asian grouping, but if this is not possible just now then he seems to feel that for the moment ASAS is better than nothing. I am sure that he is far more interested in its political possibilities than in its cultural and economic activities."

Pote Sarasin, the SEATO Secretary-General, had been advocating the establishment of a regular series of prime ministers' meetings on the lines of the Commonwealth system. Sarit said he was too busy and his English too poor. Pote Sarasin and others thought ASAS could not have a wide appeal because two of its members belonged to SEATO. "If only, it is said, the Philippines had not rushed in with public announcements whenever possible, it might have been feasible to coax Burma into coming in, and with this achieved, Cambodia might have been tempted to join because if the idea of Summit Talks had been promoted Sihanouk might well have agreed to participate."[30]

At the end of July the three Foreign Ministers met in Bangkok, and their declaration, issued on 31 July, established the Association of Southeast Asian States (ASA). Its machinery was to include an annual meeting of foreign ministers, preceded by a meeting of the joint working party; a standing committee, chaired by the foreign minister of the host country, and including the diplomatic representatives in its capital; ad hoc and permanent specialist committees; and a national secretariat in each country.[31]

For Thanat, Roger Peren reported from Bangkok, ASA was "entirely separate from SEATO — untarnished, as it were[,] by non-Asian influence — but a useful talking point when the future of SEATO is being discussed and possibly even an 'alternative in being'".[32] That its concern over Laos played a part in shaping the Thai approach is also suggested by the remarks made, "after calling for a beaker of Napoleon brandy", by Anand Panyarachun, Thanat's private secretary, in a conversation at Geneva with Fred Warner of the British Foreign Office. Thailand "could not go on for ever being dependent on outside influences". Its future lay in "a loose federation of South East Asian states pursuing a neutral but strong and independent policy". It was therefore trying to get the Association of Southeast Asian States going. "This would have to come very slowly. The Burmese and the Indonesians thoroughly distrusted it and thought it merely a manifestation of American policy. But nothing could be further from the truth; to Thailand it represented a gradual severing of ties with America."[33]

The initial proponents of the association were ironically enough soon to fall out and its survival came into question. The Tunku had also been pursuing what may at least in part be seen as another means of assuring the security of the newly-independent Federation, namely its expansion to include the Borneo states, two of which were colonies of Britain and one under British protection, and also, more reluctantly so far as he was concerned, the self-governing city state of Singapore. The Philippines election of November 1961 brought to power a President, Diosdado Macapagal, who took an interest in the claim to North Borneo (Sabah) that Filipinos based on the claims of the Sultanate of Sulu. The claim had been raised in earlier years but not pressed. But if North Borneo became part of "Greater Malaysia", it would be even more difficult to take up.

The notion of a Greater Malaysia was by no means new, but it seems likely that the Tunku took it up in 1960–61 in the context of the increasingly aggressive steps the Indonesians were taking to secure Dutch New Guinea. If, however, he hoped to foreclose their interest in securing the Borneo states, they were bound to see his action as provocative, and once they had secured West New Guinea they began what became the Confrontation of Malaysia. It was only with the destruction of the Sukarno regime that that policy was abandoned. ASEAN, as Ghazali put it, was "a development out of the pains of 'konfrontasi'".[34] But it adopted the approach and methods of ASA, which had indeed been designed at once to recognize and to contain Indonesia's primacy in the region.

From ASA to ASEAN

In September 1962 C.M. Bennett, the New Zealand High Commissioner, reported on a "remarkably blunt" speech the Tunku had given to UMNO Information Officers which referred both to Indonesian interest in the Malaysia proposal and to the Philippines claim to North Borneo. "Everybody is free to follow developments on Malaysia", as the former Indonesian Prime Minister, Ali Sastroamidjojo, had proposed, "but I must say categorically", the Tunku continued, "keep your hands out of our affairs." The Sabah dispute, he went on, was unfortunate since it might jeopardize the relationship between two ASA partners. Perhaps, Bennett thought, the Tunku was hitting a little harder than he needed, especially in respect of Indonesia. Since he had returned from the London negotiations on Malaysia he seemed to have "lost some of his urbanity, strength and elasticity".[35]

Early in November Bennett discussed the claim with the Tunku. Would he, in the light of it, attend the next ASA meeting as Foreign Minister? The claim, said the Tunku, was "foolish and frivolous". But he wanted "to do what he could to secure and preserve the future interests of ASA and towards this end he was even prepared to turn a blind eye on the obvious weaknesses and irrationalities of one of its partners". Since independence, Philippines politics had been characterized by "elements of opportunism, profligacy and inconstancy". It was only since he had brought the Filipinos "into our fold" that the "Asian limelight" had fallen upon them. "And this is how they express their gratitude." He would attend ASA, but would refuse to be drawn into the Sabah controversy. "Whether an alliance of this kind can last", Bennett concluded, "is questionable."[36]

The ministerial meeting was postponed till April 1963 as a result, as the New Zealand High Commission in Kuala

Lumpur put it, of the Philippines claim and the need for what the Tunku termed "a better atmosphere". ASA "has had a hard row to hoe and progress has been slow. Even so, before the North Borneo claim threatened to relegate the association to the ranks of other now forgotten projects at regional cooperation, it could be said that the three countries were making a serious attempt to make ASA work, and that it had moved beyond the stage of lip service to general principles." That the meeting was finally held was "a tribute to the genuine concern of all three nations, and especially Malaya and Thailand, not to allow contentious issues to mar the future of the organisation". Its achievements were modest, but it "proved the will of the three countries to preserve ASA in the face of disruptive political issues, is there, even if the way has not been found".[37]

Regionalism in Southeast Asia gives some account, drawn from such authorities as B.K. Gordon (*The Dimensions of Conflict in Southeast Asia*, Englewood Cliffs: Prentice-Hall, 1966) and Matthew Jones (*Conflict and Cooperation in South East Asia*, Cambridge University Press, 2002), of the diplomacy associated with Maphilindo and the agreement that an impartial authority should ascertain the views of the Borneo states on joining Malaysia. A summit took place from 31 July to 5 August 1963. The joint statement made reference to such Indonesian concepts as *musjawarah* or consultation and the Afro-Asian spirit. It also declared that the foreign military bases in the region were "temporary in nature", and "should not be allowed to be used directly or indirectly to subvert the national independence of any of the three countries". In accordance with the principle in the Bandung declaration of 1955

(6a), the three countries would "abstain from the use of arrangements of collective defense to serve the particular interests of any of the three big powers".[38]

Neither this nor the arrangements made for ascertaining Borneo opinion halted Confrontation. The Tunku announced on 14 September that Malaysia would come into being on 16 September. Indonesia and the Philippines announced that they could not at once recognize it.[39] Manila–Kuala Lumpur relations were severed. But the subsequent deepening of Confrontation was followed by the re-establishment of consular relations, though the Sabah claim was not dropped.

While he remained President, the Gestapu coup of 30 September 1965 brought Sukarno's career to a halt. It held out the prospect of an end to Confrontation, though the ruling triumvirate — Soeharto, Adam Malik, and the Sultan of Jogjakarta — did not abandon it at once.[40] Late in November the Thai Foreign Minister expressed his hope that ASA would be revived. The Tunku spoke of expanding it. One thing at a time, said Thanat, though Singapore — which had been extruded from Malaysia in August — would be welcome. Revival awaited a decision from the Philippines, and he spoke of mediation.[41]

There was a need for a new approach to regionalism, Foreign Secretary Narciso Ramos told the new President of the Philippines, Ferdinand Marcos, early in 1966, and his country was well suited to lead it, partly because the Asian Development Bank (ADB) headquarters had just been established in Manila. If reactivating ASA were favoured, it should be spelled out as "a transitory arrangement, a stepping stone, toward the formation of the Organization of Asian States, with a call for wider collective action to achieve Asian progress".[42]

The New Zealand High Commission recounted a conversation in March with Jack de Silva, then a principal assistant secretary in the Malaysian External Affairs Department. Indonesia had been discussed in a different context. Australia and New Zealand would be welcome candidates for ASA membership, though only in the long term. "It was thought that the organization could and should grow to take in a wider regional grouping. Indonesia must clearly be considered a potential candidate, and Australian and New Zealand participation would most usefully balance Indonesian weight and influence in the area." ASA, the Malaysians appeared to think, "should develop into a broad regional organization serving as a focus for political stability", not anti-communist, but non-communist. It might be anti-Chinese "to the extent of acting as a counter-weight to the influence in the area of mainland China. They would hope through ASA to divert the interests and energies of the overseas Chinese away from ancestral links with mainland China towards participation in the regional problems of the states in South-east Asia." In that sense, Hunter Wade thought, ASA looked like "a sort of regional projection of the [UMNO-MCA] Alliance". It might also counter any attempt by Singapore to be the focal point of the Chinese in Southeast Asia. In its own interest it would have to join, External Affairs thought, but it gave no sign of offering encouragement.[43]

Foreign Affairs in Singapore itself doubted the value of joining. Extruded from Malaysia the previous year, it was, as J.H. Weir reported to Wellington, "preoccupied in its international relations with establishing the basic infrastructure of nationhood". It would seem to be in its best interests — "and ours" — if the Singaporeans, "for the immediate future,... concentrated their slender administrative resources on these essential, practical arrangements". Off the cuff Lee Kuan Yew had told a press conference on 11 April that "he would like to know first what sort of club it was, whether it was for mutual political support, or something more solid which envisaged ultimately economic union or economic unity".[44]

The end of Confrontation was, of course, welcome in Wellington. Preparing itself for the ANZUS (Australia, New Zealand, United States Security Treaty) meeting in Canberra at the end of June, External Affairs noted that some people, "including a few Indonesians", were "toying with the idea of a new security arrangement centred on Indonesia and Malaysia". Would U.S. Secretary of State Dean Rusk see merit in Australasian participation "in order to off-set too strong an Indonesian influence? Our own feeling is that until Indonesia shows herself to be really committed to a peaceful-neighbour policy we cannot give too much weight to such ideas. We would, moreover, be concerned to prevent an isolation of Singapore by pan-Malay interests which could lead it to seek the sympathy of Communist China." Similar considerations arose in respect of a possible revival of interest in a form of political association including Indonesia.[45]

The Tunku, as the New Zealand High Commission in Kuala Lumpur reported, was cautious over the expansion of ASA. In more or less his last act as Acting Minister for Foreign Affairs, Tun Ismail by contrast went much further. "The stage is now set for full-scale resumption of ASA. There is every reason to hope for an early participation of Indonesia in a wider grouping of Southeast Asian states.... We, in Malaysia,... look forward to a regional association embracing Thailand, Burma, Indonesia, Singapore, Malaysia, Philippines, Cambodia, Laos and Vietnam." The nations and peoples of Southeast Asia had to "pull together and create, with hand and brain, a new perspective and a new framework". The ASA principles were a good starting point, but the name did not matter. Ismail envisaged "an organization which would be, first and last, pro–South-east Asia, pro-development, pro-regional cooperation and pro-peace". The Tunku was subsequently reported as saying that enlargement would be discussed at the Foreign Ministers meeting in August.[46] For him, however, the name certainly mattered.

The formal ending of Confrontation was negotiated during these months. The Indonesian Foreign Minister, Adam Malik, told reporters after meeting Razak in Bangkok at the end of May that he and the Malaysian, Thai, and Filipino Foreign Ministers had all been thinking of an association of Southeast Asian nations "which might be regarded as an expansion of Maphilindo under a different name".[47] Malik had told Michael Stewart, the British Foreign Secretary, that neither ASA nor Maphilindo "corresponded to the realities of the situation". As my earlier book relates, in August he told Paul Hasluck, Stewart's Australian counterpart, that Indonesia could not join ASA. What was needed was another body which would be an expansion involving elements of ASA and Maphilindo. Its function would be close cooperation between neighbouring countries in economic, cultural, and technical matters. "At some time it would be rather difficult to avoid discussion of defence"; but Indonesia did not want to stress that in the first place. The founder-members would be Indonesia, Malaysia, the Philippines, and Thailand. Singapore would be a member, Malik added, "though he could not yet say whether a founder-member". Indonesia could not see itself "simply stringing along with a group of South-East powers already in association", commented Horace Phillips at the British Embassy. "[B]y virtue of its size and position", it regarded itself as "the potential leader in the area and, as such, will insist on being a founder-member of some new regional grouping".[48]

In December 1966 Malik, as Michael Leifer relates, stated publicly "that Indonesia would take the lead in establishing regional economic and cultural co-operation to achieve a united South-East Asia", in which Australia and New Zealand might "eventually" take part, in order to stem what he called "yellow as well as white imperialism". Maraden Panggabean, Deputy Army Commander in Chief, declared that Indonesia must, in face of "China's ambitions in the region and aspirations towards nuclear capability", strengthen its armed forces so as to be able to join in a common defence effort with its neighbours. Malik rejected a regional military alliance as against the principles of Indonesia's national policy laid down by the MPRS (Provisional People's Consultative Assembly) — "Independent and active, opposed to imperialism and colonialism in all their forms, and participating in implementing a world role based on independence, abiding peace and social justice"[49] — and as likely to conduce to war. Indonesia took the view that Southeast Asia's security was "in the first instance the responsibility of the countries of the area themselves".[50]

Horace Phillips discussed the Singapore base with Soeharto himself. Was it still necessary now that relations with Britain had improved? Or did the British Government doubt his assurance that Indonesia had "no expansionist ambitions or aggressive intentions"? He recognized the dangers from Communist China's expansionism, but Singapore was a target for it. "The defence of South-East Asia ought to be matter for the countries of the area themselves", and if the United Kingdom and its allies helped in the supply of arms, "Indonesia could play a leading role in this". He did not expect the base to be moved "overnight", but saw it as a gradual process to be aimed at.[51]

In Kuala Lumpur Walter Ayathuray, head of the Malaysian ASA secretariat, gave the British High Commission a copy of the first draft of an agreement Thanat had sent the Tunku in December and information of subsequent exchanges. The draft, found in the British documents, was in the form of a joint declaration by foreign ministers. It began by reciting their belief that the countries of Southeast Asia shared "the primary responsibility for ensuring the stability and maintaining the security of the area from subversion in any form or manifestation in order to preserve their respective national identity and to ensure peaceful and progressive national development in their respective countries and in their region in accordance with the ideals and aspirations of their peoples". It also stated their agreement "that foreign bases are temporary in nature and should not be allowed to be used directly or indirectly to subvert the national independence of their countries, and that arrangements of collective defence should not be used to serve the particular interest of any of the big powers". Peace, freedom, social justice, and economic well-being, they affirmed, could best be attained by "fostering good understanding, good neighbourliness and active cooperation among their nations". Their conviction was that "mutual cooperation in the economic and technical fields and cultural relationship" would contribute to the welfare of their peoples and their mutual understanding.

Desiring to establish "a firm foundation for common action to further regional cooperation in South East Asia", the Foreign Ministers declared the establishment of the South East Asian Association for Regional Cooperation (SEAARC). It aimed to "promote mutual understanding[,] harmonious relations and friendly cooperation among the nations of the region", "strengthen regional peace and security", cooperate in promoting Southeast Asian studies, and generally "consult and cooperate with one another so as to achieve the aims and purposes of the association, to contribute more effectively to the work of existing international aid agencies, as well as to resolve any problems that may arise between them". It also aimed to establish an effective machinery for consultation, for "active collaboration", and for "mutual assistance in the economic, social, cultural, technical, scientific and administrative fields"; to provide training and research facilities in member countries for nationals and officials of other members; to provide machinery for collaboration in using resources, developing trade and industry, improving communications, and raising living standards; and to "consult and cooperate ... in the study of the problems of commodity trade".

Under the draft the Foreign Ministers also declared "that the association is in no way connected with any outside power or power blocs and is directed against no country, but represents the collective will of the nations of South East Asia to associate themselves for the mutual benefit of their respective peoples without surrendering any portion of their sovereignty, having as its objectives and through joint endeavour, the promotion of the well-being and the economic, social, technical and cultural progress of this region". It would adopt ASA-type machinery.[52]

The New Zealand High Commission discussed "[t]he current testing of the wind" on regional cooperation with officials in the Malaysian Foreign Ministry. It seemed to derive from "a number of factors", including "personal ambitions", United States interest in promoting stability, "the steady growth of confidence since the ending of confrontation", and "common awareness of the dangers of the Vietnam situation". Thanat's first letter was described as "a bolt from the blue", and the immediate reaction in Kuala Lumpur was that it was "further evidence" of his personal ambition. The Malaysians were "positive" that the joint declaration was drafted in Indonesia and they were not happy with the references to foreign bases. "The basic Malaysian position is that while they are no less convinced than the Thais of the necessity to strengthen regional attachments with Indonesia they are not prepared to so at the risk of weakening ASA just when that organization is recovering from three years in limbo.... They also consider that while Sukarno remains President and in the confused period which is likely to succeed his departure it is inopportune to begin institutionalizing the new relationship which they hope to build up with Indonesia." Zainal Sulong said it was necessary to proceed with caution and that was why the Malaysians had suggested the two-level approach. If "satisfactory progress" were made in the larger group, it would "subsume" ASA, and an expanded ASA or SEAARC would be established. A wider Southeast Asian group might follow.

The New Zealanders had also spoken to Benny Moerdani, Indonesia's emissary in Kuala Lumpur. He "seemed to think that Indonesia would gain automatic entree to the regional 'club' and be accepted as the leader of the drive for cooperation. The Army was anxious to press ahead, and would welcome the participation of countries other than the core grouping." He was not explicit about foreign bases. "He recognized that a United States presence would contribute to stability for a long time to come, but hoped … that the countries of the area would work towards their own security arrangements." Zainal thought the references in the draft declaration "could only have been an Indonesian smoke screen". The declaration must have been Indonesian in origin, and Thanat had "accepted to carry the ball further forward".[53]

Anwar Sani, Director-General of the Indonesian Foreign Ministry, told Phillips that the draft was generally acceptable to Malik "because it made it clear that the proposed regional co-operation did not extend to defence", so that Indonesia "no longer had inhibitions about going into formal association in other fields even though its partners … might have bilateral defence arrangements with Western powers". In deference to "Army thinking", he had been required to write into the Siamese draft "something to the effect that foreign bases in the area must be regarded as temporary". Malik and he did not want to pick a quarrel with the army on the issue, Sani told Phillips, "though they still believed that the soldiers aim was to try to build up the strength of the armed forces on the pretext that South-East Asians (given a lead by Indonesia) should be able to defend themselves and thus get rid of foreign bases". That, Malik and Sani thought, was "unrealistic, besides being undesirable from the domestic point of view".[54]

Soeharto's chief political adviser told the New Zealand legation in Jakarta that Panggabean was a "second rater", but, judging from the remarks he had made to Phillips on Singapore, Edmonds thought that Soeharto fundamentally sympathized with his point of view. Malik, Edmonds added, had to work through army ambassadors in almost every Southeast Asian capital. "No doubt one reason he wishes to keep the initiative in promoting an organization for regional cooperation is to maintain his own control over a vital area of foreign policy and to build up the power and prestige of the civilian side of the government as opposed to the military." If the initiative were successful the generals would go along with it "as a move which increases Indonesia's influence and standing". It should he helpful, the New Zealand Chargé felt, in "providing a framework within which Indonesia can constructively cooperate with its neighbours and obtain some legitimate outlet for its hegemonic impulses".[55]

In Manila Foreign Secretary Ramos told the Commissioner for New Zealand in Hong Kong that his government was "still strongly attracted to the concept of an expanded ASA — Malaysia, Thailand and the Philippines, plus Indonesia.... not necessarily under the same name. It would have the same objectives as ASA 'plus political overtones'."[56] Ramos told J.M. Addis, the British Ambassador, that the plan was to form a new association, "a merger of ASA and Maphilindo under a new name", taking "the best points from both". While the countries of the region would still look to the United Kingdom and the United States for "the main defence, they also needed to include some security aspect in the new association, since in the future the countries would have to look to some extent to their own defence". The Philippines wanted Singapore to join, but Malaysia should have "first say" on that.[57]

In mid-April Malik declared that plans were going ahead for a new organization and the Tunku declared that Indonesia could join ASA, "We already have our regional economic grouping."[58] But at a meeting with Thanat on 20 May, according to MFA officials, the Tunku "surprised everybody" by changing his line, as my previous book relates. Officials could not explain the Tunku's about-face, "except possibly in terms of recent reports of increased Philippine interference in Sabah", including alleged attempts to encourage secessionism. But Bentley thought it "equally possible" that the Tunku saw no point in maintaining ASA "once an essentially parallel organization had been set up".[59]

The five Foreign Ministers held informal discussions at Bangsaen, then drove to Bangkok, "rewrote" the draft, and issued the ASEAN declaration on 8 August 1967. Press reports indicated that the preambular statement attracted most controversy during the discussions. The resulting declaration modified the ex-Maphilindo "Thanat" draft to read: "foreign bases are temporary and remain only with the expressed concurrence of the countries concerned and are not intended to be used directly or indirectly to subvert the national independence and freedom of states in the area". Malik remarked after the meeting that Indonesia left it to the countries concerned to determine how long bases would remain. "The statement concerning collective defence arrangements that served the interests of big powers was", as Roger Irvine points out, "conspicuous by its absence."[60]

Zainal Sulong gave the New Zealand High Commission an account of the discussions on his return. While the Ministers, other than Malik, played golf, officials devoted two days to the two principal issues: the references in the draft to internal security and the temporary character of foreign bases. "The discussion was arduous." Thailand and the Philippines had made large concessions on these issues to the United States, and Singapore and Malaysia wanted to retain a British presence. Indonesia was "anxious ... to demonstrate that the new organization would not be merely another military pact nor a sort of South-east Asian Trojan Horse for the influence within the region of outside powers". The Thais, Zainal thought, were "insouciant about the real meaning of the phrases regarding foreign bases which they had proposed". The Filipinos, by contrast, felt "compelled to dilute the texts as much as possible", and were "inflexible and prickly".

The Singaporeans wanted the organization "as much as possible to have the character of a practical economic grouping in which Singapore would play an appropriately hard-headed and central part. When it became clear that the others envisaged something with a broad political framework from which an attempt might be made to establish a larger political organization", they were "reluctant to proceed". When it became clear that references to internal security and foreign bases would be included, Singapore "insisted that its proposals for regional cooperation be tacked on as a special and separate memorandum of understanding". Zainal thought it was "unrealistic" for Singapore, having earlier stood back, to "come in at the last minute … with specific plans for cooperation, particularly since many of them had already been undertaken in ASA", while others were "impracticable".

The Philippines draft included a provision from the Manila accords of 1963 that international relations in the area be conducted in conformity with international law. The Malaysians were "naturally suspicious" that that was "a backhanded attempt to introduce the contention that the Sabah claim should be considered at the International Court". Eventually they secured a redraft included in the main declaration indicating that the association would "promote regional peace and stability through abiding respect for justice and the rules of law in the relationship among countries of the region and adherence to the principles of the United Nations Charter". Zainal thought that "would sufficiently confuse the issue and remove any obligations over the Sabah claim". Ramos, it was felt, had to come back to Manila "with a piece of paper demonstrating that the establishment of ASEAN had not prejudiced the Philippines' hopes in Sabah". In fact

there was renewed resentment of the Philippines in Kuala
Lumpur, Zohrab reported, the Tunku being "particularly
bitter" at its "irresponsible" pursuit of the claim.[61]

Before the meeting, Weir reported from Singapore,
it was already clear "that the Singaporeans had in large
measure got over their wariness of association with their
neighbours". Their emphasis was, however, on "concrete"
proposals, a joint shipping line, cooperation among rice-
producing countries, and "rationalisation of industries".
The Malaysians were critical. But the Singaporeans were,
Nathan (Assistant Secretary for Policy, MFA) told the
New Zealanders, "reasonably satisfied" with a clause in
the communiqué which left the standing committee to deal
with proposals for regional cooperation in tourism, trade,
shipping, and fisheries. Nathan said they had not been
"happy" with the preamble's reference to members' determination "to ensure their stability and security from external
interference", but were alone in their opposition and finally
agreed to its inclusion. "Singapore has for a long time
been anxious that regional cooperation should not take on
a political hue, not necessarily because it could appear as
a pro-Western development but because it does not think
the political base is the right one for association." Nathan
"did not foresee Indonesia obtaining an undue permanent
dominance in the club".[62]

The Commissioner for New Zealand in Hong Kong
spoke to Ramos and to the Under-Secretary for Political
Affairs, Pablo Pena. "They seem happy enough about the
way things worked out. A measure of compromise was
reached on the bases and security clauses which they
had considered unacceptable, and in any event they now

seem to feel that there is no cause for concern about the understanding between the five foreign ministers on those counts." Razak gave them no support, but, with Singapore's help, "the outcome was satisfactory". At one point in the discussion about the bases clause, according to Pena, Malik said that the Indonesians were not worried in the slightest about the "bases of the free world". Their only concern was the possibility of Chinese or other communist bases. He gave the Filipinos the impression "that he was not without fear about the possibility of closer relations between Singapore and mainland China at some time in the future". Over Sabah, Pena said, the Philippines position was "protected and had been well covered in the exchange of notes when diplomatic relations between Malaysia and the Philippines were resumed".[63]

Political considerations were "played down", but were, as Irvine puts it, "of primary importance". The principles in the preamble themselves suggested "at least the rudiments of a common political programme for the association", and it was acknowledged from the beginning that political matters were discussed in private sessions.[64]

Even before the Bangkok meeting, officials in Canberra concluded it was obvious that the Malaysians had "changed their attitude towards the prospect of a new regional body". "Earlier misgivings about Indonesia's intentions and capacity for harm seem to have been subordinated to the more urgent need of not foregoing the opportunity, through regional arrangements, of drawing Indonesia into harmonious and constructive relations with its neighbours." Economically, it was thought, there were "severe practical limits to what the five countries can do together". The importance of ASEAN was "more in the political than economic sphere". In promoting a new organization, "Indonesia was seeking to exert a leading role, thereby restoring some of her self-respect and what she regards as her rightful place of pre-eminence in the region. Such expansion is likely to take place in any case because of Indonesia's size, population and potential economic and military strength. However, ASEAN may prove useful in providing a framework for orderly and peaceful development in this direction."[65]

Copied to Wellington, this assessment probably influenced the New Zealand Department's appraisal. That, too, suggested that the political significance of ASEAN was greater than the economic. It had the advantage of including Indonesia, unlike the other regional groupings. It provided "a context within which Malaysia can achieve a satisfactory relationship with Indonesia, something it has been striving to obtain ever since the end of confrontation. At the same time Indonesia's preponderant influence is moderated and contained by other members, especially Thailand." ASEAN should also "help end Singapore's isolation by fostering an atmosphere in which it can work out a satisfactory relationship with Malaysia and Indonesia. At the same time Thai and Filipino pressure should limit any excessive pan-Malay pressure which might otherwise bear over-heavily on Singapore."[66]

The New Zealand documents, along with the British, throw some light on the negotiations that led to ASEAN. The Tunku obviously questioned whether or not Indonesia would be adequately contained within an organization in the founding of which it had taken a lead. For Malik it was essential to take that lead, countering the unrealistic and undesirable aspirations of the army. Newly-independent Singapore was nervous about the political implications of an agreement that involved its two neighbours. It resolved to take part and to emphasize the economic functions of the association, from which indeed it stood to benefit. The Thais seemed to take a larger and more long-term view, though the Malaysians commented on Thanat's personal ambition. The Philippines claim to Sabah had, to the Tunku's fury, not been abandoned and, as it had damaged ASA, so it was to damage the early years of ASEAN, which was predicated on the acceptance of current boundaries. ASEAN might indeed not solve such issues. It could and did prevent their escalation, and though there might be differing reasons for joining an association, that did not prevent its taking on a life of its own.

ZOPFAN

ZOPFAN, the Zone of Peace, Freedom and Neutrality in Southeast Asia, was another Malaysian initiative, advanced at a time when Britain had withdrawn the bulk of its forces from the region and the United States had begun to come to terms with the People's Republic of China. The archives in Wellington, like those in London, help to document the concept. Tun Ismail, former Minister of Home Affairs and advocate of regional association,[67] had in fact presented the idea in a debate on defence in the Dewan Rakyat back in January 1968, his aim being to save money that could be spent on social services. "The time is ... ripe for the countries in the region to declare collectively the neutralization of South-East Asia. To be effective, the neutralization ... must be guaranteed by the big powers, including Communist China ... it is time that the countries in South-East Asia signed non-aggression treaties with each other. Now is also [the] time for the countries in South-East Asia to declare the policy of co-existence, in the sense that the countries in the region should not interfere in the internal affairs of each other and [should undertake] to accept whatever form of government a country chooses to elect or adopt."[68] The Tunku did not think the time had come, but Abdul Razak, his deputy, thought the concept "wise, imaginative and far-sighted",[69] and he came to power after the 1969 riots in Kuala Lumpur.

In a speech in July 1971 Prime Minister Razak argued that the involvement of major powers was the essential reason Southeast Asia had not been at peace for twenty years. Peace and security could be safeguarded only by "a policy of neutralisation which will ensure that this region will no longer be a theatre of conflict for the competing interests of the major powers". That required that the states in the region had to "work to bring about the conditions which are necessary for the realisation of the neutralisation proposed and show that a neutralised Southeast Asia meets the basic legitimate interests of the great powers themselves". Malaysia's "vision" was of "a Community of Nations.... When we look at the map of Asia, it is possible to see that Southeast Asia is a clear and coherent unit which through the vicissitudes of history has not been able to play its proper part in the world."[70]

In October 1971 Ghazali bin Shafie of the Ministry of Foreign Affairs published a defence of the proposal and outlined the steps Malaysia envisaged for implementing it.[71] At the first level, he argued, the individual countries of the region must "respect each other's sovereignty and territorial integrity, and not participate in activities likely to directly or indirectly threaten the security of another. Non-interference and non-aggression are basic principles which Southeast Asian countries must unequivocally accept before any further steps can be taken." All foreign powers were to be "excluded from the region", which "should not be allowed to be used as a theatre of conflict in the international power struggle". The countries of the region should ensure peace among member states, and present "a collective view before the major powers on vital issues of security" and "promote regional cooperation".

At the second level, the three major powers had to agree that Southeast Asia was "an area of neutrality", and "undertake to exclude countries in the region from the power struggle amongst themselves". They should "devise the supervisory means of guaranteeing Southeast Asia's neutrality in the international power struggle. Just as the Southeast Asian countries will be responsible, under the neutralisation plan, for maintaining peace among themselves, so will the guaranteeing powers be responsible for preventing externally-inspired conflict in the region."[72]

The ASEAN Foreign Ministers met in Kuala Lumpur on 26 and 27 November 1971 and signed a declaration announcing their agreement "that the neutralisation of Southeast Asia was a desirable objective" and that they should "explore ways and means of bringing it about". The preamble alluded to UN principles, the Bandung conference of 1955, and the Bangkok declaration of 1967 that had founded ASEAN, and took cognizance of the move towards nuclear-free zones in Africa and Latin America. The declaration itself stated that Indonesia, Malaysia, the Philippines, Singapore, and Thailand were "determined to exert initially necessary efforts to secure the recognition of, and respect for, Southeast Asia as a Zone of Peace, Freedom and Neutrality, free from any form or manner of interference by outside Powers".[73] A joint communiqué indicated that the ministers would encourage other countries in Southeast Asia to associate themselves with the declaration and would establish a committee of senior officials "to study and consider what further steps should be taken". Great powers and guarantees were not mentioned.

The New Zealand High Commission in Kuala Lumpur had been clear that it would be difficult for the five countries to reach agreement on the items on the agenda of the meeting. Malaysia wanted the goal of neutralization to be accepted "as completely and unambiguously as possible", but did not consider it was opportune to try to coordinate the countries' policies towards China, and thought President Marcos' concept of an Asian summit would damage the development of ASEAN and neutralization. Thailand was hesitant about neutralization, preferring "a watered-down 'declaration of South East Asia as a zone of peace'". Indonesia was "sceptical of Malaysia's ideas and fearful that they would drag the region precipitately into Peking's arms. In particular, Indonesia opposed the 'Great Power guarantee' idea, preferring that the region's security be guaranteed from within rather than from without. There were hints that the Indonesians were the only delegation even prepared to contemplate an eventual ASEAN military alliance.... The preponderance of senior military men in the Indonesian delegation ... indicated that the Indonesian military leadership did not quite trust Malik not to become infected with the Malaysians' enthusiasm." Singapore stressed the need for existing relationships to continue until neutralization was "an accomplished reality".

Officials began discussions on 25 November, before them a Malaysian paper on neutralization, an Indonesian one on relations with China, a draft declaration of neutrality prepared by the Thais, and a general review from Singapore. Only at a social function with the Ministers in the evening did the atmosphere grow positive. "'We got all the Ministers sitting on sofas together and let bonhomie take over', a Malaysian official told us later."

Officials were subsequently instructed "to concentrate on hammering out a Declaration dealing with the *goal* of neutralisation, and to forget about the divisive issue of the *means* by which neutralisation was to be achieved", and they were told that there had to be documents which all could endorse. "This display of 'good jokerism' enabled a fairly bland Declaration and Communique ... to be hatched."

The Declaration was "vague, harmless", the New Zealanders reported, showing "how low the meeting had to go to achieve unanimity". In the phrase of the Japanese Ambassador, it was like a drink in a hotel lounge: "very little whisky and a lot of fizzy water". But it had "something for everyone". Agreement to hold an ASEAN summit in Manila saved Philippines face. "The Singaporeans were catered for by the establishment of an officials' committee to define and give scope to the meaning and content of neutrality." The Indonesians knocked out any reference to great power guarantees. "Malaysia has the references to the goal of neutralisation to show for her efforts." Thailand's phrase "a zone of peace" had its place in the declaration.

The Malaysians professed not to be "disheartened.... They say they expected no more and are content that a start has been made. 'The essential achievement of the meeting', a high Malaysian official told us, 'was collectively to express the long range objectives of the five ASEAN countries with reference to the promotion of stability and security in South East Asia.'" Razak told a press conference that the Declaration indicated that the Southeast Asian countries were determined to shape their own destiny. "Malaysia expects it to take a good few years for any neutralisation of the region to be within its grasp", but "feels ... that the steps that have been agreed as necessary to keep up momentum are definite enough to be adequate".

There was no reference to a great power "guarantee", but Malaysian statements continued to refer to it as "a final stage of the process of securing neutralisation". Reports from Moscow suggested that the government there saw it as "an American-inspired manoeuver". The Malaysian Secretary-General of Foreign Affairs thought neutralization would "suit China's book". The Australians had been concerned that they were excluded from a major initiative, but dropped a notion of sending up a senior official to be "in the corridors".

The Kuala Lumpur Accord, R.M. Hutchens concluded, showed that the five ASEAN nations were prepared "to address themselves as a group to the problem of the future political shape of the region". What emerged was "general and watered-down", but could be used "as a basis for the 'five' to feel their way towards something more solid". Whether it would be so used was less certain. "The meeting represented their first collective effort to grapple with the shifting Asian power-balance. The chances are that the Kuala Lumpur Accord will not get written up in the history books as a milestone, but if it does, it may appear there as marking the genesis of a 'South East Asian bloc'."[74]

The fifth ASEAN Ministerial Meeting was held in Singapore in April 1972. The communiqué, as the New Zealand High Commission reported, noted that ministers reviewed international developments that made it necessary more than ever for ASEAN countries to cooperate. That was "an oblique reference" to an agreement reached on 14 April that ministers should, as proposed by the Singapore Foreign Minister, S. Rajaratnam, convene once a year to discuss international developments. Such meetings "would be outside the purview of ASEAN and would preserve their informal character". The Permanent Secretary of the Singapore Foreign Ministry would not say what had been discussed, but the inference was that they had covered Chinese policies in the region. "He still maintained the old line that ASEAN was 'not a political organisation'."

The meeting on 15 April dealt with neutralization. The Malaysians circulated two papers. One set out a programme of action designed to give substance to the concept of Southeast Asia as "a zone of neutralisation", no reference being made to "a zone of peace, freedom and neutrality", and included a series of questions on the role ASEAN, as at present or enlarged, might play in developing the concept. The second contained the text of a model treaty drawn from a book by Falk et al. written "three or four years ago" on ASEAN neutralization. The Malaysians suggested that officials should discuss their papers at a meeting in Kuala Lumpur in May. The other four delegations preferred to prepare their own papers. "Our informant commented that the Malaysians, while urging action, seemed less determined than previously. He wondered whether they, having already gained considerable mileage among the 'non-aligned' nations but receiving 'a fairly rough time' from the Indonesians in the process, might now prefer to hasten more slowly."[75]

Singapore had traditionally opposed any attempt to give ASEAN a political role, the High Commissioner commented, "on the grounds that accord would be difficult to reach, and would risk rending the agreement already obtained on economic objectives". But Rajaratnam "had concluded that the trend started late last year with the talks about China's entry to the United Nations, the agreement to consult each other before pursuing relations with Peking, and the November meeting in Kuala Lumpur on neutralisation, and continued more recently in the discussion of Bangladesh recognition could not be halted and should, in some flexible fashion, be institutionalised". The ministers met in private, without advisers, on the matter. The Singapore MFA had included in the draft statement only one paragraph, "simply noting the agreement to meet at least annually". That was not enough for Malaysia and the

Philippines, and the final declaration referred specifically to the Kuala Lumpur declaration and communiqué.[76]

The Thais, the New Zealand Embassy in Bangkok reported, did not seem "as concerned as some others that these political meetings should be outside ASEAN's formal framework, but neither are they troubled by the artifice". Foreign Ministry officials were concerned over American policy, the Chargé added. The United States was "engaged in a global policy of withdrawal and it is prepared to see, at least in South East Asia, the expansion of Communism rather than intervene directly to prevent it"; it was, "in view of at least some Thai officials, a rather unreliable ally". Thai views on neutralization had to be put in that context. Thanom told visiting members of the U.S. War College that neutrality was "an empty concept: if China is involved, he said, there can be no guarantee that the commitment will be honoured; if China is not involved, there can be no guarantee at all." Foreign Ministry officials held out more hope; "They are less convinced that the Chinese, despite their support for insurgency, nurse expansionist aims in South East Asia and have not failed to notice the gap between Chinese rhetoric and action. They see the objective as a worthwhile one and the road ahead as being long and difficult but they are prepared to explore seriously any option that holds a promise of long-term security while retaining for the present established alliances."[77]

In Wellington the Ministry prepared an account of the development of the proposal and commented on its prospects. The neutralization of Southeast Asia was an idea that was "superficially attractive" and might have "some real merit", but was "extraordinarily difficult to put into practice". The involvement of the area in great power politics arose from divisions and conflicts within it, and while those persisted, there would always be incentives for the great powers to intervene. If they agreed to guarantee its neutrality, "it would almost certainly be in the hope of playing a larger part in its affairs, and the result would probably be the reverse of what was intended". It was not an objective that New Zealand could at that stage endorse or advocate.

It was, however, "desirable that the countries of the area should work more closely together and take more responsibility for the security of the area. It is also desirable that they should think out for themselves the reasons for their involvement with the great powers and their inability to achieve the goal of neutrality." The proposal was already serving a useful purpose "in giving the Malaysians an incentive to talk more to their neighbours, including Singapore, about the security problems of the area, and to take their views into account". In the longer term there might be more scope. "If and when a negotiated settlement is reached in Indochina, and that area is to some degree neutralised, and if the arrangement proves durable, there may be some possibility of extending it [to] cover the whole of South-east Asia. But the 'if' are big ones, and the 'may' is very tentative."[78]

Many miss the point, the Canadian High Commission suggested, that the Malaysian Government was not promoting neutralization for tomorrow "but rather for an indeterminate date in the future when the United States' role in this part of the world has diminished, the five power defence arrangements are over and China, Japan and

Indonesia are exerting the major influence in the region". Razak, the Commission noted, had spoken in the past of guarantees, but the Declaration used the words "recognise" and "respect". The Malaysian Foreign Ministry spokesman "indicated that the use of 'recognize' was calculated and meant to imply the recognition of Southeast Asia's neutrality in the same way that all recognized Switzerland's neutrality. To 'guarantee' the area's neutrality could imply a role for the super powers to police the guarantee and presumably the countries of the region do not wish this." Malaysia did not see a military pact as a result, but it did not rule out "the possibility that at some future date when all or nearly all the countries of the region have adhered to the declaration and the neutrality of Southeast Asia has been recognized (guaranteed) one country might request the military help of another or even several others if its neutrality is threatened by outside influences". Such issues would be discussed when officials met.[79]

At that meeting, held in Kuala Lumpur from 6 to 8 July 1972, Malaysia produced a detailed paper, including a draft treaty. That took the others aback and it was decided to focus on the "initial steps" to which the Declaration had referred. A working group defined "peace", "freedom" and "neutrality" and the meaning of a "zone of peace, freedom and neutrality". There were differences over "neutralisation", used in the preamble of the Declaration. Was it the end or the means to an end or a means to the end? The Malaysians, as *Regionalism in Southeast Asia* relates, were asked to reformulate their ideas.[80]

A meeting of Foreign Ministers was held in Manila the following week. After it, Carlos Romulo of the Philippines told the Australian Ambassador that neutralization had been the main topic. It was seen, he implied, as one means towards establishing the zone. "Asked to distinguish between 'neutrality' and 'neutralisation'", he said that "neutrality was that condition under which a state maintained its independence of, and impartiality towards, the great powers. Neutralisation was the condition of a neutral state whose status was guaranteed by the great powers." He agreed "that it could be argued that neutralisation, on this definition, derogated from the independence of the neutral state and that it was hard to see how it could be a means to the end goal of neutrality". As for other means of attaining that goal, Romulo spoke of the possibility of a unilateral declaration being made by the ASEAN countries that they constituted a zone of "peace, freedom and neutrality".

Romulo thought it might take ten to fifteen years to reach the goal. "Essentially he regarded the exercise ... as a form of contingency planning." The ASEAN countries "had to prepare for the eventuality that the United States no longer maintained bases in the region and agreements between, for example, the Philippines and the United States and the five power arrangements had been phased out". With respect to disputes among member states, they were "aiming to establish a situation akin to that now existing among the countries in Western Europe, i.e. the exclusion of war as a means of resolving their differences". Their harmony was already substantial, and Romulo played down Sabah as a source of friction.[81]

The Australian High Commissioner in Kuala Lumpur thought the meeting had been a setback for the Malaysians, but they were determined to push ahead. At the Ministry Zainal said they wanted to have something in place when the defence agreements came to an end. "It was also urgent because of the whole way things were moving, the development of the United States/China relationship, events in Korea, with the latest contacts between north and south, and in particular Vietnam." There was an opportunity that might not last "to develop a regional agreement which could secure endorsement and support from the great powers". The High Commissioner questioned whether great powers would live up to statements they made. It was clear that Zainal had China in mind, and "felt that, unless progress could be made towards securing statements of good behaviour from the Chinese which would provide a 'guaranteed norm' for Chinese behaviour and which could lead, if contravened, to counter-intervention by the great powers, if so asked by the Southeast Asian state or states concerned: then each country would be left to make the best deal it could with China — in the absence of any real American support post-Vietnam."[82]

Officials met in Jakarta in December. They "sought to establish the principles on which neutralisation should be set up and to consider the ways of promoting the conditions in which a zone of peace would prosper and survive", Albert Talalla of the Malaysian Foreign Ministry said. "They ... succeeded in establishing a code of conduct for states both within and outside the region and they had made some progress on lines of action for the promotion of the zone."[83] The report did not refer to great power guarantees, but that, the New Zealand High Commission in Singapore later learned from a MFA official, Goh Kian

Chee, did not mean that the idea had been abandoned, but that the current focus was on the zone.[84]

The Paris settlement of the Indochina war in February 1973 made Zaiton (Secretary General, Malaysian MFA) "optimistic" that "neutralisation" might be established in the region "sooner than many people believed", the New Zealand High Commission in Kuala Lumpur reported.[85] In mid-April Zainal indicated what Dr Ismail planned to say at the ministerial meeting in Pattaya: "that while the expansion of ASEAN has great potential, uncertainties in Indo-China render it premature".[86] Laos and the Khmer Republic sent observers. North Vietnam refused and South Vietnam declined at the last moment. The meeting agreed on the need to hold a meeting of all Southeast Asian nations. "Ministers hoped", the New Zealand Embassy in Bangkok reported, "that by spelling out publicly the objectives of the conference and by emphasizing that ASEAN felt 'animosity towards none' North Vietnam would be encouraged to come to the party in time. But there is no expectation of an early response nor of an early conference." Much the same was to be said about expansion of membership. "The conference is seen as a first step towards the ultimate enlargement of ASEAN but the point is taken that neither the conference nor any expansion can precede a firm political settlement in Indo-China." The ASEAN Ministerial Meeting (AMM) endorsed the guidelines on neutralization that the officials had worked out in Jakarta in December. The next meeting of officials, the New Zealand Embassy reported, would address the question of great power guarantees: "Are these needed, and if so in what form? Will they not give the great powers the excuse to meddle in the affairs of the region? And so on."[87]

The follow-up meeting of ASEAN officials on neutralization was held at Baguio from 19 to 21 June 1973. In Kuala Lumpur the desk officer, Azzat, told the British that delegates had expressed differing views about the "guarantees", some wanting them carefully defined, others happy with "a purely token expression by the super-powers of their recognition and respect of the concept of neutralisation". The Malaysians were somewhere in between; "They wanted guarantees to be meaningful but not so firm as to give any of the super-powers the right of intervention." They were not "disheartened" by the Baguio meeting. Neutralization was still being discussed. "They have never expected anything other than a long haul on neutralisation and the success of the policy may be seen to lie not so much in its eventual fulfilment but in the sense of direction and the cooperation among ASEAN countries which it promotes."[88]

"The aspiration is", as Sir J. Johnston, the UK High Commissioner in Kuala Lumpur put it, "that at some time in the future the association will extend to include the other five SE Asian countries: and that together the Ten will form an area of 'peace, freedom and stability', collectively persuading the super powers to remain at a political equidistance which none singly could hope to achieve." No one in Malaysia thought that enlargement or neutralization were "on the discernible horizon". They might never happen. But they were "a present convenience", providing "an immaculate set of foreign policy objectives now, to which neither East nor West can object".

My previous book reproduced some of Johnston's penetrating analysis. "Faced with the prospect of an assortment of SE Asian States, appearing in the aftermath of one or another kind of colonialism, disunited, uncertain and obvious take-over targets — the classic 'power vacuum' after British, French and partial U.S. withdrawal — the Malaysians believe that the regional acceptance of the common policy goals they have described as neutralisation will give the region the appearance and possibly a genuine sense of direction and unity of purpose, and strengthen its position vis-à-vis the super powers." They believed, perhaps rightly, "that if these aims and objectives are sufficiently reiterated and successfully put across, they may possibly derive from their acceptance as objectives some of the benefits that in theory would flow from their eventual realisation".[89]

Students of international relations sometimes draw too firm a line between realism and constructivism. This was a realist's constructivism. By talking in a particular way, you were also acting, in a sense bringing about at least part of your stated objectives. Among contemporary officials, Johnston seems to offer the keenest perception of ASEAN diplomacy. New Zealand comments, though not at odds, were rather less sharp.

The reference the New Zealand High Commissioner in Singapore made to the "book by Falk et al." is presumably a reference to *Neutralization in World Politics* by Cyril E. Black, Richard A. Falk, Klaus Knorr, and Oran Young, published by Princeton University Press in 1968, following on their report to the Senate Foreign Relations Committee of 10 October 1966. It includes documents on the neutralization of Laos in 1961–62 and also the "draft outline of a model treaty of neutralization" (pp. 191–95). That was concerned with a single state, and it provided for guarantors (p. 193). Malaysia had initially sought guarantors in the ZOPFAN discussions. In a sense ASEAN's regionalism was, however, a substitute for them. If neighbours did not fall out, there would be no need to call in outside help. Still more significant, though less obvious, was ZOPFAN's multi-state aspect. In this declaratory and constructionist kind of diplomacy, numbers would count. The Laos negotiations may again be relevant. At the time Prince Sihanouk — in the event vainly — suggested a neutral belt in Southeast Asia, covering at least his country and neighbouring Laos. The British Foreign Office saw advantage in it: "it enshrined the 'Sacred Cow Principle'", as Fred Warner, head of the South East Department put it. "It was easy enough for powers to knock around a little ping-pong ball like Laos but once you had established a neutral belt this became a major feature of the world political scene and it would be considered a great sacrilege to tamper with it."[90] Recognizing the principle, the Malaysians were to be more ready to drop the difficult question of guarantees.

The Summit

The seventh ministerial meeting was held in Jakarta, 7–9 May 1974. The counsellor in the Singapore Embassy told the Australians that "the major agreement reached had been on agreeing to disagree". They were told by Adenan of the Indonesian Ministry that the Philippine proposal on the formal machinery for settling disputes had not been well received. "Malaysia wanted first the zone of peace. Indonesia did not want formal machinery linked with great power guarantees." ASEAN should produce its own machinery, "and the Indonesian way was to do this by informal bi-lateral or tri-lateral contacts whenever necessary". For the sake of unanimity, the press statement referred to the Philippine proposal as being accepted in principle.[91]

The New Zealand High Commission in Kuala Lumpur reported the views of Under-Secretary Talalla, who had been at the meeting. He agreed that economic progress was slow, but that 'was bound to be the case, since the organization included no countries with large resources of expertise or capital. He "was inclined to place greater emphasis on the political value of Asean and on the political aspects of the recent meeting.... There was now a well established mutual concern to preserve harmony." The High Commissioner thought that was shown by the Philippines' readiness to stand down their offer to host the proposed secretariat and by the deferment to Malaysia's sensitivity over the settlement of disputes. The Philippines had proposed establishing appropriate "machinery". "This could have been interpreted as implying the establishment of a rigid system of referral to a tribunal or court of arbitration and it caused the Malaysians some disquiet, particularly because of their long-standing difficulty with the Philippines over the problem of Muslim insurgency. The Philippines agreed to change the term to 'procedures'." Officials, said Talalla, still had to work out the details and then ministers would examine the proposals.

The New Zealand officials referred to the improved situation in Laos, where a Provisional Government of National Union had been formed.[92] Would Laos now become a member of ASEAN? The timing, Talalla responded, was "not right.... it would be desirable for Asean to retain its membership as it was at present and to expand to full potential membership in one fell swoop. This would give Asean, as it now existed, time to consolidate and would also avoid a situation in which late starters for membership could feel that they had been left out in the cold. If this is, in fact, the accepted approach it is likely to be some time before Asean membership changes."[93]

In Singapore Goh Kian Chee, a member of the delegation to Jakarta, told the New Zealand diplomats that his country was "generally well satisfied with the outcome", and pleased at a re-emphasis on economic cooperation. Little had been achieved politically. "We asked whether the differences between Malaysia and the Philippines had affected the proceedings. Goh said there had been an underlying atmosphere of suspicion — 'tension would be putting it too strongly'. He thought Indonesian efforts to mediate had only a slight chance of success — the Malaysians weren't particularly interested, and the differences ran too deep for an outsider to heal. The Indonesians were galvanized by a real fear that the dispute could wreck ASEAN, which they now considered as a most important and convenient stage from which to play the larger role in regional affairs their size warranted." Goh agreed that Indonesia was the leader of the group and the sitting of the secretariat confirmed that. He speculated that Indonesian domination, "if too obvious", might put the North Vietnamese off. Expansion of membership had been discussed "only generally", he said, but "did not trot out the usual 'all in at the same time' formula". The most serious difference that emerged was over the "machinery" question.[94]

Early in 1974 ASEAN had initiated a discussion with Australia on the subject of aid, and the secretaries-general were invited to visit Australia. The Secretary of Foreign Affairs suggested to Prime Minister Norman Kirk that they might be invited to come to New Zealand.[95] The way towards New Zealand–ASEAN cooperation was not smooth, however. Yusof bin Ariff of Malaysia insisted on a formal approach.[96] Moreover, the Philippines felt unable to agree to closer cooperation while New Zealand was unrepresented in one of the ASEAN capitals, Manila.[97] The opening of a post there should remove the obstacle, Wellington declared in August 1974.[98] Its formal establishment was required, however.[99] The Filipinos adopted the stance, it was reported, not because it was offended, nor because it wanted to force New Zealand to open an embassy, "but rather because they believe to acquiesce now could establish a precedent for subsequent modifications of [the] basic Asean tenet of equality of all members to which they attach particular value. They have said, for example, they would have to oppose closer association of Asean with Burma or Papua New Guinea if this also entailed inequalities, including resident representation."[100]

Late in October, however, it was possible to start discussing cooperation with Yusof. New Zealand thought in terms of supplying trained personnel rather than capital.

"Yusof was lukewarm in his reaction. 'Let's be honest', he said. 'Political strategy is the basis of these ASEAN projects. As such, they must be visible.'"[101]

No doubt, the Singapore mission wrote, the New Zealand Government would be seeking ideas from the ASEAN partners. It ought, however, to outline some possible projects if only to indicate the scale it thought appropriate and the nature of the relationship it envisaged. "As to style, we take it that you would prefer to make maximum use of New Zealand expertise and world-wide contacts, concentrating on brain power and organizational ability, and to limit the input of man-hours or capital." But what was the broad thrust of New Zealand's policy? "While we have no plans for a 'United States of Southeast Asia' we are, surely, attempting to nudge the ASEAN countries towards regional thinking and towards management of their resources on a regional basis. The long-term goal is closer integration. Essentially we would like to strengthen the region so that it will be able to withstand economic storms and the pressures of the great powers — and in due course of North Vietnam. This means that the Southeast Asians must be helped to make the best use of their resources of food, energy, raw materials and manpower. We have to encourage them and also to show them how to think regionally." It might be possible to devise projects like "Planning and Management of Regional Forest Resources" or "Planning and Management of Regional Energy Reserves". They need not be costly: the New Zealand contribution would be "brains, know-how and imagination, not large amounts of capital". New Zealand might have to give in to pressure for one or two high-profile "quickie" projects, but it should keep its priority clear.[102] Wellington thought that geothermal and forestry projects were ruled out because of other calls on New Zealand manpower.[103]

The sudden collapse of the regimes in Phnom Penh and Saigon in April 1975 caught ASEAN countries "unprepared", Irvine suggests.[104] At the eighth AMM, held in Kuala Lumpur from 13 to 15 May 1975, Razak "adopted the most conciliatory response". He expressed a "fervent hope" that the countries of Indo-China would join in building "a strong foundation of regional co-operation and regional peace". The founders of ASEAN had envisaged that it would eventually include all the countries of Southeast Asia. "When I look at the map of the world, I see Southeast Asia as a cohesive and coherent unit.... Surely the moment has come for that community of Southeast Asia, which has been our dream, to be realised?"[105]

Singapore was more "circumspect", as Irvine puts it.[106] Rajaratnam also "urged ASEAN countries to make their decisions on the basis of a continuing Western presence in the region".[107] Malik evoked Bandung. Adjustment to the new situation should not be inspired by fear, nor by perceived vacuums in power relationships. "He proposed instead a framework of power relationships based on the Bandung principles of peaceful coexistence, noninterference, respect for sovereignty and territorial integrity, equality and justice".[108] In their final statement, the Foreign Ministers expressed their willingness to enter friendly relations with the Indo-Chinese countries and to cooperate in "the common task of national development", but made no mention of expansion.[109]

The meeting agreed to accept for consideration by governments a draft treaty of amity and cooperation. "This was hailed as an important step towards the realisation of the Zone of Peace, Freedom and Neutrality. It was moreover noted with satisfaction that progress was being made by Senior Officials in working out a 'blueprint' for the Zone."[110]

The Thai Foreign Minister proposed "a forum of all Southeast Asian countries ... to discuss and settle differences between the communist and non-communist states", but the prospects for such a forum "quickly faded" with skirmishes on the Thai-Cambodian border and between Vietnam and Cambodia over islands in the Gulf.[111] Malik took up a proposal, made earlier by the Philippines, for a meeting of ASEAN heads of government. During a tour of other capitals, Kukrit, the new Thai Prime Minister, secured the agreement of the other leaders.[112] A "flurry of meetings" preceded the summit,[113] including the first-ever meeting of Economic Ministers, held in Jakarta, 26–27 November 1975.

On 14 January the New Zealand High Commission in Kuala Lumpur discussed the meeting of Foreign Ministers scheduled for 8–9 February with Yusof Hitam (SEA, MFA), who had been at the officials' meeting in Manila the previous week. He said the summit would see the signing of the treaty of amity and also endorse the approach towards ZOPFAN. He expected the communiqué to reiterate the ASEAN governments' willingness to enter into friendly relations with the Indo-China governments. Looking to the future, he said, ASEAN governments did not foreclose any possibility for securing their cooperation, "even if this should mean the replacement of ASEAN by a new organization (just as ASA was replaced by ASEAN to bring Indonesia into the fold). He said that this possibility had not been discussed, but it had to be borne in mind."[114]

The British Embassy in Jakarta considered what Indonesia hoped to achieve at the summit. They seemed, as General Adenan confirmed at MFA, to be looking at it "principally as a symbol and expression of political will to make greater progress in the Association in the future". They hoped it would produce a Bali Declaration to replace the Bangkok Declaration, to finalize the treaty of amity and cooperation, to issue a number of declarations of intent, and probably to initiate discussion on security and defence matters.

Malik had told the press on 30 January that the summit would issue a "Bali declaration", making "the Heads of Government level the highest instrument of the Association". It would confirm the political role of ASEAN and, so the desk officer in the MFA in Jakarta told the British Embassy, "touch on security matters". The treaty of amity and cooperation, "intended to provide a formal framework for the solution of conflicts within ASEAN", was, the embassy understood, ready for signature. Agreement on ZOPFAN was, however, unlikely to be formalized. Because foreign forces remained in ASEAN countries, General Adenan said, it was "too soon to make progress". Nor had the question of outside guarantees been settled, he said, though the Deputy Chief of the Malaysian mission had told the British that his government might be dropping their insistence on them.

Public comment had been focusing on economic cooperation. Indonesia was unwilling to accept a free trade area until its industries were developed, and the remarks of Malik and others on the matter had angered the Singaporeans. The Indonesians, the British understood, were still discussing cooperation on security and defence matters, but recognized the reluctance of Malaysia and others to move towards it. They considered that it was too soon to consider enlargement to include the Indo-China countries, but had expressed "hopes of useful co-operation, in the field of exchanges of technology, for example".

The Foreign Ministers, A.C. Stuart concluded, would have plenty to do at their pre-summit meeting if the Heads of Government were not to "spend valuable time hammering out remaining differences of opinion and emphasis". But even if they were not resolved, and no concrete ASEAN policies emerged, the summit would have been useful "in forcing the member states to look much more closely at the practical possibilities for economic and political co-operation".[115]

Senior officials meeting in Manila worked on the draft declaration of cooperation and solidarity that the Foreign Ministers endorsed at Pattaya on 9 and 10 February in a meeting that in fact lasted but three and a half hours, the Australian Embassy in Bangkok reported. "The exercise was largely one of consolidation, of devising formulae and finding wording which was generally acceptable.... The expressions on consensus in the document seem to constitute a lowest common denominator of agreement. Even so further work in refining the text remains to be done before the summit." Under-Secretary Anand and

Thai Secretary-General for ASEAN, Jet N., gave Johnston information of its contents: reference to internal security, though no machinery of cooperation is mentioned; defence cooperation, seen as a bilateral matter; reference to ZOPFAN, the treaty of amity, which was being looked at again by Hussein Onn's new Malaysian Government, and to the settlement of differences between members. There was a general reference to the liberalization of trade, but none to specific projects. "Jetn attached importance to a statement of policy concerning the raising of living standards of rural populations and in narrowing the gap between agriculturalists and city dwellers. Progress in this field was regarded as important for maintaining internal stability and security."[116]

The results of the Pattaya meeting were also discussed by the Australians in Singapore. Desker, the Principal Assistant Secretary SEA at MFA, who had been a member of the delegation, said that Singapore was "broadly satisfied". The potentially divisive question of multilateral defence arrangements had been overcome, even the Indonesians now recognizing "that defence cooperation should be conducted at a bilateral level in order to avoid unnecessarily antagonizing the Indo-Chinese states". The Indonesians, too, were at least prepared to talk about economic matters at Bali. "There had been problems, however, with the treaty of amity. The Malaysians were now claiming that they could not yet give assent to the document, largely, Singapore suspected, because of Marcos's references during his visit to Singapore to the treaty's possible use in reaching a solution to the Sabah problem." The Australians asked whether the communiqué would refer to Timor, which Indonesia had invaded in December. Desker said Singapore hoped not. "Indonesia could not expect Singapore to acquiesce in any attempt to obtain formal ASEAN endorsement of its actions there. On the other hand, Singapore could not object to more general references to the right of member countries to protect their own territorial integrity."[117]

Besides the meeting of Foreign Ministers, there had been meetings among the leaders. A mini-summit — Singapore, Thailand, and the Philippines — took place at Razak's funeral. Lee subsequently met Kukrit and was visited by Marcos and Hussein. Hussein also went to Jakarta and Bangkok. The Australians in Singapore commented on the Republic's policies. It remained, Birch said, "apprehensive about its place within the area encompassed by Malaysia and Indonesia". In his talks with Hussein, Lee expressed his concern that Malaysia was not dealing with communist terrorism effectively and that its bumiputra policies were divisive and destabilizing. Singapore's relations with Indonesia were currently "troubled". Lee had tried to cultivate Soeharto during 1974 and 1975. But now Indonesia's Timor policy had put Singapore in a no-win situation.

Singapore had "minuscule intrinsic interest" in Timor, but had "identified an important interest in the *way* in which Jakarta has conducted itself and the likely impact upon the Jakarta polity of the Timor issue. It feels threatened by (and indeed resents) an Indonesia which seems to take for granted regional approval of its actions: by the prospect that the Timor policy might signal a turn towards increased militarism in Jakarta: and by the implications, with respect to possible Malaysian designs on Brunei, of an uncriticised or unrestrained Indonesian incorporation of Timor." It thus abstained in the UNGA vote on the Timor issue, angering Jakarta. It had since expressed "disquiet" over trends in Jakarta and there had been "whisperings" about Soeharto's "losing his grip". Bali should provide an opportunity to resolve such concerns, but Timor would remain "a central problem". Hussein had apparently reassured Soeharto that Malaysia had "no qualms" and other states voted at UNGA. But Indonesia would probably try to obtain summit endorsement of the view "that each member must continue to protect its own integrity as the basic means through which regional security is maintained. Such a general statement would have the twin virtues of a variety of national interpretations, and the utility for Suharto of its being able to be represented as acceptance of his Timor policy." Singapore would probably offer no objection.

"A key issue in the wider development of ASEAN is the relationship of member countries with the United States." Singapore wanted a U.S. presence off-shore in Asia. "Equally it wants greater definitional clarity of the United States policy of remaining 'just over the horizon'." It had, however, made it clear "that it would have reservations about the United States making Indonesia the 'sheet anchor' of its South East Asian policy. It does not want the United States to moderate its relations with ASEAN through its bilateral relations with Indonesia."

ASEAN incorporated both "a shifting set of national interests" and "a cluster of common interests". The adjustment of the former and the development of the latter would be affected by the modus operandi that emerged in ASEAN and at the summit. Singapore relied largely on "the western business ethic of negotiation through offer and counter offer". Other members tended in varying degrees to adopt "a Malay-Javanese method in which a special form of politeness, a tendency to say to others what it is thought they want to hear and will not cause embarrassment, is more usually the norm". Like the *wayang kulit*, "this approach casts images larger than life which are merely projections of figures manipulated anonymously behind a screen". It also raised the question, "as yet unanswered in ASEAN", which leader or government would emerge as "the director of the play". It might not therefore be easy to know soon after Bali whether, "irrespective of the visible show,... adjustment of various interests has in fact taken place and common steps forged". Possibly the problems would be too hard and a shadow play would be "substituted for commitment".[118]

The Australian High Commission in Kuala Lumpur talked to See Chak Mun, counsellor of the Singapore High Commission there, about the Pattaya meeting, which he had attended. He confirmed that the Malaysians were unhappy with the treaty of amity and indeed in a mood not to sign it. "He agreed with our suggestion that the reason was Malaysian anger with a recent statement of Marcos to the effect that the Sabah dispute was an example of an intra-regional dispute that could be dealt with by the machinery provided for in the treaty. Malaysia had not been the originator of the treaty of amity (a Filipino idea) but had gone along with it as a means by which implementation of the ZOPFAN could be facilitated.

However, Marcos' recent remark had made them feel they were being led into a trap." The Malaysians, See said, were still incensed by Marcos' behaviour when he visited Kuala Lumpur for Razak's funeral. He had participated in a mini-summit that excluded Malaysia. He had also behaved in an inappropriately publicity-seeking manner and gone out of his way to meet Tun Mustapha.

The Indonesians, See said, now accepted that there should be no reference in the summit communiqué to multilateral security cooperation. "The Indonesian attitude appeared to be that all that mattered now was that there should be a declaration that would be known as 'the Bali Declaration', which could be cited along with the Bangkok Declaration and the Kuala Lumpur Declaration. They did not seem too fussed about what the content of it was — it would all be in very general terms anyway."[119]

The British Embassy in Bangkok also reported, somewhat frustratedly, on the FMM in Pattaya. "All meetings were in restricted session, and the whole affair was remarkable for the amount of disinformation disseminated at all junctures", but some further indications of the likely format of the Bali Summit emerged. Divergent opinions on economic development appeared even before the meeting began. Rajaratnam spoke strongly in support of an ASEAN Free Trade Area, Rithaudeen took a more cautious line, and Romulo said it would not be raised at all. There were long hours of discussion among senior officials, ending with "an apparently much watered-down draft on general economic cooperation". The main opposition was apparently Indonesian. After the Ministerial meeting, officials seemed to do their best to fudge their countries' position. Rajaratnam, however, spoke unequivocally of Singapore's disappointment.

On political matters Ministers answered questions "in terms so general and anodyne as to be nearly meaningless". But the meeting appeared to have considered a strategy paper proposing a constructive approach to the Indo-Chinese countries on the basis of the Bandung principles, each country being treated separately. Its salient points would be included in a Declaration of Cooperation and Solidarity. Anand, the Thai Under-Secretary, said its main aim was to "institute a regional identity, regional cooperation and regional solidarity". Press leaks suggested it would be "a kind of 'ASEAN bible'".

Security was "[a] very touchy subject". Ministers and officials were clearly concerned "to avoid giving any impression that ASEAN was about to 'gang up' on the communist governments in Indo China". There was nevertheless some discussion of security, "covered with an even thicker blanket of obfuscation than other topics". Rumour had it that Singapore and Indonesia circulated a memorandum "suggesting overall joint security efforts for the suppression of insurgents along the common borders of the ASEAN countries". The difficulties in that were "self-evident".

The British Ambassador called on Anand on 17 February. The treaty of amity would be signed, he said, and a declaration would probably be issued. Nothing new would be said about ZOPFAN and "nothing very concrete" about economic cooperation. It was wrong to expect concrete results from the summit. What was important was that it was taking place. "This in itself was a measure of the greater solidarity that was developing."[120]

Marcos and Kukrit had been reported as favouring an invitation to the leaders of Japan, Australia, and New Zealand to talks with ASEAN leaders post-meeting. Malik had told Yoshino that it would be discussed at Pattaya and that he was in favour. Japan did not look for any special relationship and Miki was looking rather for an informal exchange of views. It was, however, likely that the meeting of ASEAN and JANZ (Japan, Australia, New Zealand) leaders would "generate a special atmosphere of warmth and friendship that would be generally helpful later". If it attended, Japan would express support and indicate interest in any ASEAN project. "Japan does not wish to see Chinese/Russian domination of the ASEAN countries and therefore seeks through its presence to convey psychological and spiritual support", Yoshino told the New Zealand Embassy in Tokyo.[121] Khor Eng Hee of the Malaysian MFA said no consensus existed and he thought nothing would come of the idea.[122] According to the British, Malik made plain his view "that Bali would not be the best occasion for such a regional gathering". The President apparently spoke to Hussein Onn on the same lines and he said there was "no urgency" for the non-ASEAN leaders to go to Bali.[123]

The idea was indeed turned down at Pattaya.[124] The decision not to invite Japan and Australia, Birch suggested, was influenced, like other decisions, by the concern "to avoid ASEAN being seen by the Indo-China countries as SEATO Mark 2".[125] Prime Minister Muldoon had thought it would be unfortunate if New Zealand were overlooked,[126] but did not wish to attend if the meeting would be of as little substance as Yoshino suggested.[127] According to the British, the Japanese and Australians, however, "demonstrated extraordinary interest" in the Pattaya meeting. "The Australian Ambassador himself booked into a Pattaya hotel with his family. He told the press that he was observing the Meeting in a private capacity." But he was quoted — admittedly in a newspaper "with a reputation for spectacular inaccuracy" — as saying that Chatichai had been "quite positive" on the matter. Perhaps the Thais were surprised at the outcome. "The rebuff to Japanese and Australian hopes was short, sharp and mishandled": the Chairman declared that the heads of government would have to leave Bali early on 25 February and so the Australian and Japanese Prime Ministers could not meet them. It was difficult not to see that as a snub, the British commented, "possibly arising from the carefully concealed divisions which have plagued the preparatory meetings for the Summit".[128]

Nothing startling emerged from the Foreign Ministers' meeting, Tan Boon Seng told the New Zealanders in Singapore: they rubber-stamped the decisions the officials had taken. The focus had been on the declaration. What it would say on economic cooperation had still to be settled, and perhaps for that reason Tan would not give the New Zealand officials a copy of the documents. There was little prospect of agreement on establishing a free trade zone, but Singapore was working to ensure that the principle of cooperation was accepted. The other main item had been the treaty of amity, the Malaysians having difficulty over the section dealing with the settlement of disputes. Fraser and

Miki had not been rejected, Tan said: the Foreign Ministers had not received a formal request for an invitation. Because of press comment they had been obliged to consider the matter. In the event, because at least two of the heads of government had to return home immediately after the summit, a meeting in Bali was not on. "Tan did not rule out the possibility of a meeting at a later stage but we got the clear impression that, at least for the moment, internal ASEAN matters are the over-riding preoccupation." There had been no reference to New Zealand.[129]

It seemed unlikely, the New Zealand High Commission in Singapore commented — rather in the style of their Australian colleagues or the British in Jakarta — that the summit would be "either a great success or an obvious failure". There would be "an appearance of agreement, suitable words will be found for the communiqué, and both the participants and interested observers such as New Zealand will have to wait some while to find out what — if anything — it all meant". The meeting might itself be seen as a useful step forward. Perhaps the most positive move would be the setting-up of the secretariat, though a Jakarta-based secretary-general (Dharsono) was "unlikely to put much effort behind initiatives not entirely acceptable to the Indonesian hierarchy". The Singaporeans would be disappointed. After the fall of Saigon they had worked harder than ever to move their partners to take a step towards "a more modern-minded economic grouping". They must be wondering whether their effort was wasted. "On what might be called the strategic side they are likely to seek to get a little closer to the United States, whatever their ideas about maintaining 'balance'."[130]

In Jakarta too, the New Zealanders expected "neither dramatic progress nor acrimonious disagreement, but there is no point in talking about 'success' or 'failure'. The Bali meeting's significance is that it is happening at all. A kind of coming of age party for ASEAN." The paternity of the summit idea had been "variously ascribed", but the Indonesians had been the leading proponent over the past nine months. None of the members were "bursting with enthusiasm". But it developed "a sort of momentum of its own".

Indonesia would not move far, if at all, towards the free trade area concept. It was not merely technocrats who were opposed. "Commitment to industrialization and job creation through industries protected from outside competition is a basic element of Indonesian government policy. And the Timor vote issue has once again showed the strength of the lurking Indonesian envy and resentment of Singapore's prosperity and drive." The rationalization of industries on an ASEAN-wide basis and joint ASEAN-established new industries were equally unlikely to advance.

The documents that would emerge — the treaty of amity, the declaration, the guidelines for ZOPFAN — would not be "much more than window dressing". What the leaders said publicly and privately about the Indo-China states "should be more significant". Even given Indonesia's "coolness", it seemed likely — and it was "certainly desirable from New Zealand's viewpoint" — that the summit would publicly make "friendly noises". The Indonesians had "backtracked somewhat ... on their various kites about greater security cooperation". But it was still "an Indonesian objective to give meaning to regional resilience in the sense of ASEAN solidarity against outsiders, and in current circumstances to try to stiffen the backbone of the Thais in particular. (... the almost missionary zeal of the Indonesians in urging regional resilience seems to be related less to a real current capability to help their partners, than to a sense of 'manifest destiny' about Indonesia's long term leadership role in SE Asia which their partners must at times find hard to take)." The Ambassadors had been invited to Bali for the opening of the summit, "the Indonesians laying on special flights simply to have us there for a couple of hours, as part of a no-expenses spared extravaganza".[131]

In Kuala Lumpur the Australian High Commission secured a briefing at Wisma Putra on the new Prime Minister's attitudes to foreign affairs and on Malaysia's approach to the summit. He was not as committed to ZOPFAN as Razak had been, it gathered, nor had he done as much thinking on regionalism. "He believes, however, that ASEAN should operate quite informally and by consensus. He does not support intraregional schemes of economic cooperation if these have to be pressed on some members against their real wishes, even if it might be for the greater good." He relied heavily on Tan Sri Ghazali Shafie for advice. Ghazali's approach to foreign policy was one of realpolitik and he was also the negotiator with the Indonesian and Thai armed forces, e.g., in the border committees. There were no formal links between Ghazali and the Foreign Ministry, but he kept in close touch with many of his senior officers, who felt "a closer affinity with him and his thinking" than with Foreign Minister Rithaudeen. The last indeed came "a poor third" in shaping

Malaysia's policy. Hussein Onn's commitment to Islam was stronger than Razak's, the Australians learned. That coloured his view of the Middle East crisis and also of Thai and Philippine treatment of Muslim rebels. "From the point of view of a Malay Muslim, Marcos is not 'sincere' and thus cannot be trusted, and so long as that feeling persists there is not likely to be any improvement in Malaysia/Filipino relations." The speech that was being drafted for Hussein would include a little of Razak's conceptual doctrine and of Ghazali's realpolitik, but would be "low key and fairly pragmatic".

The Malaysian Cabinet, the Australians were told, had made the mistake of assuming that the treaty of amity was "an instrument to formalise the processes of ASEAN". It had in fact been originally conceived as "an instrument for preparing the way for the implementation of the ZOPFAN, and indeed some of the ZOPFAN language had appeared in the original preamble". The Filipinos had managed to have most of that removed, "arguing to the effect that you could not have a treaty based on a proposal that had not been fully defined nor accepted by the non-ASEAN South East Asian states". Malaysia had let that pass early in 1975, "but recent statements by Marcos had led the Malaysians to fear that unless there were adequate safeguards written into the treaty, it could be used by the Philippines as a way of imposing on Malaysia a requirement to have the Sabah claim (which Malaysia regards as dead) arbitrated upon by ASEAN machinery". Attempts were under way to ensure that safeguards were written into the treaty to ensure that it did not become part of the ASEAN machinery.

Singapore, officials confirmed, was likely to press for
the inclusion in the communiqué of something firmer on
economic cooperation than the present draft contained.
"Malaysia had not liked what Lee Kuan Yew had attempted
to do at the mini-summit meeting in Kuala Lumpur last
month, and also did not want to push Indonesia into
something it was not ready for." Its basic objective at
the summit was to obtain endorsement of ZOPFAN. Not
much would be made public, however, until it had been
discussed with, and approved or amended by, Burma and the
Indo-China states, and further considered by ASEAN.[132]

The Malaysian Cabinet, the New Zealand High
Commission reported, reacted strongly to a statement
on Sabah that Marcos made in Singapore. Rithauddeen
made it clear at Pattaya that Malaysia would not sign the
treaty unless safeguards were written in. "In essence, the
Malaysians want it made crystal clear that the treaty does
not impose on ASEAN members a binding obligation to
submit bilateral disputes to the organization for settlement."
Officials were dealing with the issue at their pre-summit
meeting in Jakarta. "The Malaysians are apparently
confident that they will get what they want. But if the
Filipinos dig their toes in, it may well be that the treaty,
at this stage, may simply take the form of a statement of
principles."[133]

The British Embassy in Jakarta had thought that the
treaty of amity and cooperation would go through without
difficulty. "There has, however, been a row about it which,
according to the Indonesians, at one stage threatened the
Summit itself." That related to the settlement of disputes.
Malaysia feared that the Philippines might acquire the

right to "a say in the future of Sabah, and similarly [the Philippines feared?] that Malaysia could gain a *locus standi* in Philippine problems with the Muslim extremists". Suffri Jusuf, the Indonesian Director of Legal Affairs, who described himself as the author of the draft treaty — "others say the Philippines drafted it", an FCO (Foreign and Commonweath Office) official noted — told Stuart that at one stage Indonesia told its partners that if the dispute weakened or destroyed ASEAN "this would be no skin off Indonesia's nose, since Indonesia could survive without ASEAN". He implied that his tough talk brought the others to their senses, and that the treaty would be signed but without the protocol or schedule dealing with the settlement of disputes. "We shall see."[134]

The Treaty of Amity

The treaty as concluded at the summit meeting, 23–25 February, covered the "machinery". The preamble alluded inter alia to the desire "to enhance peace, friendship and mutual cooperation", consistent with the UN Charter, the ten principles of Bandung, the Bangkok declaration of 1967, and the Kuala Lumpur declaration of 1971. Article 1 declared that the object was to promote peace, amity and cooperation, and Article 2 that the parties would be guided by the principles of "a. Mutual respect for the independence, sovereignty, equality, territorial integrity and national identity of all nations; b. The right of every State to lead its national existence free from external interference, subversion or coercion; c. Non-interference in the internal affairs of one another; d. Settlement of differences or disputes by peaceful means; e. Renunciation of the threat or use of force; f. Effective cooperation among themselves."

The parties agreed to promote mutual understanding and cooperation, and to collaborate (Article 6) "for the acceleration of the economic growth of the region in order to strengthen the foundation for a prosperous and peaceful community of nations in Southeast Asia". The parties were "to strengthen their respective national resilience in their political, economic, socio-cultural as well as security fields in conformity with their respective ideals and aspirations, free from external interference as well as internal subversive activities in order to preserve their respective national identities" (Article 11). They were also to "cooperate in all fields for the promotion of regional resilience, based on the principles of self-confidence, self-reliance, mutual respect, cooperation and solidarity" (Article 12).

Articles 13–17 covered the pacific settlement of disputes. Article 13 required the parties to have "the determination and good faith to prevent disputes from arising". If they did, they were to refrain from force or the threat of force and to settle the disputes through friendly negotiations. "To settle disputes through regional processes", Article 14 prescribed the setting up of a High Council, a continuing body comprising a representative of each of the parties to the treaty, "to take cognizance of the existence of disputes or situations likely to disturb regional peace and harmony". In the event that no solution was reached through direct negotiations the High Council was, under Article 15, to recommend appropriate means of settlement, or offer its good offices, or, with agreement of the parties in dispute, "constitute itself into a committee of mediation, inquiry or conciliation". That provision was not to apply unless the parties to the dispute agreed, but under Article 16 that would not prevent parties to the treaty not party to the dispute "from offering all possible assistance to settle the said dispute", and parties to the dispute were to be "well disposed" to such offers. Nothing, said Article 17, precluded recourse to the modes of peaceful settlement prescribed in the UN Charter, Article 33(1). But parties to a dispute were "encouraged to take initiatives to solve it by friendly negotiations before resorting to the other procedures provided for in the Charter of the United Nations." The treaty, signed by Indonesia, Malaysia, the Philippines, Singapore, and Thailand, was, Article 18 declared, "open for accession by other States in Southeast Asia".[135]

The Heads of Government also approved a Declaration of ASEAN Concord, by which they agreed inter alia to consider initial steps towards obtaining recognition of and respect for ZOPFAN and to strengthen "political solidarity by promoting the harmonization of views, coordinating positions and, where possible and desirable, taking common actions". They also adopted a plan of action put up by the meeting of Economic Ministers and covered, in very general terms, cooperation over social development, population programmes, and narcotics control. The Declaration also stated — "allaying fears about incipient militarism" — that there should be a "continuation of cooperation on a non-ASEAN basis between member states in security matters in accordance with their mutual needs and interests".[136] A communiqué instructed Economic Ministers to begin discussion on a detailed programme of action.[137]

It would be "difficult to reconstruct the precise sequence of consultations and meetings, changes of programme, postponements and cancellations, and apparently fortuitous conversations on the golf course", the New Zealand High Commission in Singapore commented. "It has been a hectic few days." It was clear, however, that the Foreign and Economic Ministers "only just managed to put together a package for the Heads of Government", and the latter were to meet again in Kuala Lumpur on 8 and 9 March. It seemed that Singapore found the form of words that enabled Malaysia to go along with the treaty of amity, "their acquiescence being obtained 'virtually with minutes to spare'".[138] The treaty was subjected to "[a] rapid scissors and paste job", the British noted, as was evident from its repetitive wording.[139]

Hussein Onn told the press on his return from Bali that the treaty was a major step towards ZOPFAN. ASEAN would approach the big powers, Burma, and the Indo-China states as the next step towards ZOPFAN. To be workable the concept had to win the support of the big powers: the super-powers caused the tidal waves, he said, the instability. ASEAN had extended the hand of friendship to the Indo-China states and awaited their response. ASEAN, he reiterated, was a non-ideological, non-military grouping. The meeting enabled the Heads of Government to get to know each other better. "What was more vital to make ASEAN permanent was the participation of its people in its activities."[140]

Before the summit meeting itself, the Canadian Embassy in Jakarta (Johnston) reported, the Economic and Foreign Ministers had met and Soeharto himself had met ASEAN Heads of Government in an effort to solve the outstanding problems on economic cooperation and "machinery" for settling disputes. The latter, which the Malaysians feared would enable the Philippines to resurrect the claim to Sabah, was dealt with by Article 16, providing that the machinery would not apply unless all the parties agreed to its application. The declaration of ASEAN concord was "a rambling patchwork of ideas reflecting separate interests of all 5 countries", but it laid out a programme of action in the economic and other fields. The communiqué spelled out some of the projects that could be considered, and the Economic Ministers were to meet again in March. "Although essentially cosmetic in nature [the] result has been [a] promising first step towards genuine cooperation among ASEAN members, particularly in economic matters where their interests overlap if not conflict. Now that political direction has been given by heads of government it will be more difficult than it has been for one country to put its own interests ahead of common interests of all members."[141]

At the FCO in London, as Lynton Jones put it, "any sign of progress in regional cooperation in South East Asia is a good thing" from the British point of view. "The importance of the ASEAN Summit is that it took place at all."[142] He thought that the communiqué that set out the agenda on economic cooperation for the Economic Ministers was "perhaps the most significant development". ASEAN was "initially conceived as a vehicle for economic cooperation", he wrote, but so far it had achieved little in that field. Singapore, supported by the Philippines and Thailand, had wanted the summit to consider a document agreed among them that would commit members to preferential trading agreements and tariff reductions. Malaysian and Indonesian "misgivings" meant that it was not tabled, but thanks to Singapore's pressure the summit recognized the need to move more quickly on economic cooperation. "[T]he fact remains that Indonesia regards herself as being less well-developed economically and thus less able to indulge in the sort of measures being promoted by Singapore. Rapid progress on the economic front cannot be expected."

Given the long build-up and the press leaks there were few surprises, Jones observed. There had, however, been a real possibility of disagreement over the treaty of amity and over economic cooperation. "These problems were successfully resolved at the meeting. Most member states have therefore come away from the ASEAN Summit feeling that they have achieved something." Outside the region reactions were generally favourable. The Chinese press had reprinted editorials from Southeast Asian newspapers praising the summit, though "China's current bilateral relations with Indonesia over Timor will probably prevent her from being too glowing about the Summit". The Soviet Union had reportedly offered "a tentative welcome". Hanoi was the exception. *Nhan Dan* accused the United States of mounting the summit as a prelude to "new schemes of intervention and aggression".[143]

In Singapore, Peter Ricketts of the British High Commission called on Barry Desker, who had attended the officials' meetings and the summit itself. Singapore, he said, was pleased with the decision to promote industrial cooperation: "it was better to have compromised and gained this limited agreement than to have pushed too hard for tariff cuts and risked a breakdown in the negotiations". Ricketts detected some disappointment over the lack of real progress on trade liberalization. The treaty of amity and cooperation was, in Singapore's view, "more important for its political than its legal implications", Desker said. The Philippines and Malaysia had been "persuaded to agree on a form of words to cover the peaceful settlement of border disputes: such an agreement would have been most unlikely in any other forum." ASEAN officials would now be working out the details of the economic agreement and also considering "how to develop political cooperation with the EEC [European Economic Community]".[144]

On 8 March Rajaratnam gave a briefing at their request to representatives of the Nine. The conclusion of the war in Vietnam meant that the Indo-China countries would "start to take an interest in South-East Asia", he said, and ASEAN had to review its policy. Indonesia, he said, had "viewed the situation as one of conflicting blocs". Singapore and Malaysia had thought rather in terms of "competition". If Vietnam saw ASEAN as in conflict with the Indo-Chinese states, Hanoi would be "more militant". Only with difficulty, Rajaratnam said, was Indonesia brought to agree with this approach. Once it did, it was accepted by all that economics would be ASEAN's "weapon". It was also important to minimize the differences among the ASEAN states such as those between Malaysia and Thailand and the Philippines and

Malaysia; unless a way could be found to resolve them "without open clashes", ASEAN could not progress nor "defend itself against Indo-Chinese-promoted revolution and subversion". None of the countries wanted to be responsible for the breakup of the summit, so compromises were achieved at the eleventh hour. Hanoi might now try to foment trouble in the ASEAN countries; at Bali, Rajaratnam said, "the lines had been drawn between communism and non-communism". The Soviet Union backed the Indo-Chinese states and China was therefore likely to sympathize with the ASEAN states. If ASEAN prospered, he thought, it would act as a magnet for Laos and Cambodia.[145]

The Australians in Kuala Lumpur discussed the results of the summit with Yusof Hitam, Under-Secretary for Southeast Asia in the MFA, who had participated in all the preliminary officials' meetings. He said Malaysia was very satisfied: it had secured summit support for its ZOPFAN proposal and achieved an amendment to the treaty of amity that ensured that the principle of "consent" was applied to the disputes machinery. "Malaysia was also pleased that the Summit had endorsed Malaysia's policy of presenting an open and flexible approach by ASEAN towards the states of Indo-China."

The summit, Yusof said, had amalgamated the Bangkok Declaration of 1967 with the Kuala Lumpur Declaration of 1971, and carried their "basic elements" a little further. He expected that a meeting would be held — perhaps in conjunction with the next FMM in Manila in May/ June — to work out the best means of securing a UN resolution to endorse the zone. "Some attention would also be given to the drawing up [of] a draft treaty to secure the denuclearization of the zone, which was one means of helping to exclude great power military presence or pressures in the zone." A non-aggression pact might now be unnecessary in view of the signature of the treaty of amity. Another essential step towards implementing the zone was acceptance by Burma and the Indo-China states. No technique for seeking this had been decided upon. Any ASEAN member could test the reaction of any of them. If there were general agreement, ASEAN might then make a collective approach. Yusof, the Australians noted, was soon to become Ambassador in Hanoi, and the task of "selling" ZOPFAN to Vietnam could fall to him.

The most important achievement of the summit, Yusof felt, was the treaty of amity. Members were "being asked to take a 'reasonable, calculated risk' of committing themselves to codes of behaviour and methods for the settling of disputes which they had not hitherto done". That put regional interest a little ahead of national interest and meant that bilateral disputes would not simply be set aside. Future disputes — but not past ones, like the Philippines' claim to Sabah — would be dealt with by the High Council. There would be no compulsion, however, so the "calculated risk" was "a fairly low one".

ASEAN leaders, Yusof said, decided not to act as a bloc vis-à-vis the Indo-China states, since that would be "unnecessarily provocative", be "counter-productive" in respect of ZOPFAN, and "be ineffective because ASEAN did not possess sufficient strength". Now, however, was not the time to encourage the Indo-China states to join ASEAN: some matters would be "awkward" to discuss in their presence; and their approach to industrial projects would differ. "It was thought better to let the states of Indo-China settle down further and get over some of their old 'hang-ups' before participation in ASEAN." But an Indo-China state could participate in one ASEAN activity and build up its involvement step by step.[146]

A member of the UK High Commission talked to Ben Harun of the Malaysian MFA (Assistant Under-Secretary). The Bali Summit had gone "as well as could be expected". There had been no real difficulties. That over the disputes machinery in the treaty of amity had been a "manufactured" dispute. "Marcos had been 'rather naughty' and had put his officials in an awkward position, since they had already agreed on a satisfactory arrangement. Ghazali Shafie had also played his part in hotting up the atmosphere."

The two also discussed the meeting of Economics Ministers, held soon after the Summit (8–9 March 1976) in order to respond to the need for "some *detailed* achievements". The four joint projects they agreed on were in fact already in existence. "A free trade area was not on the cards for a long time to come, but the habit of talking about economic matters was a good one to have started." For the next two to three years, Harun thought, ASEAN would develop primarily as an economic grouping. Another grouping would develop round Hanoi, "and one must hope that the two groups would then draw closer together". The hopes of closer political ties with Hanoi had been disappointed.[147]

Richard Woolcott, who had chaired the Canberra meeting of Secretaries-General and was now the Australian Ambassador in Jakarta, was in Bali for the opening.

He concluded that the summit established the "political will" and the institutional framework that would make ASEAN "more than a forum for commendable rhetoric about regional collaboration". Some of the impetus for its progress came from the communist victories in Indo-China. "[T]he future stability of the ASEAN region now clearly rests to a greater degree than ever before in the hands of the governments of non-communist South East Asia themselves."

Woolcott offered another — and more dramatic — account of the diplomacy that immediately preceded the summit. Marcos' implied suggestion in Singapore that he might use the treaty of amity to solve the Sabah dispute prompted Hussein Onn to refuse to sign it as drafted. Soeharto decided to save the summit by "a dramatic gesture": he sent secret envoys to the two capitals, Ali Murtopo to Kuala Lumpur and Yoga Sugama to Manila. The Malaysians drafted a protocol excluding Sabah from the treaty and made their signature dependent on it. On Soeharto's instructions, Yoga Sugama conveyed that to the Filipinos and told them that if they did not agree "Indonesia might not be able to 'hold back' Malaysia from involvement in the Southern Philippines dispute". Marcos made counter-proposals and also rewrote the ASEAN Declaration claiming that it was legally a bad draft. "He is said to have called his draft a Concord. Lee Kuan Yew took advantage of the confusion to push his economic proposals, including a proposal for a mutual 10% tariff cut."

Soeharto was "angered.... A successful Summit was of importance to him, both for his standing in ASEAN and for his position in Indonesia. He saw no reason to change the draft previously agreed." Woolcott thought that ASEAN leaders had understood that the Sabah dispute would not be raised under the treaty. The Foreign Ministers formulated possible solutions by the evening of 21 February, though the Philippines had not accepted them. A new Article 16, apparently a suggestion of Rajaratnam's, would require the parties to a dispute to agree to the application of the treaty machinery. The word "Concord" was added to the title of the declaration. The economic issues would be covered by the general provisions in the declaration, with the more specific points in the communiqué to be discussed by the Economic Ministers in March. "Active diplomacy by Indonesia was required to get the approval of President Marcos." Lee decided "not to press his proposals to the bitter end".

Scheduled to arrive in Bali after the other leaders, Marcos decided to arrive before them on the 22nd. "Soeharto, suspicious of Marcos' intentions, had Ali Murtopo spend most of the day with Marcos to prevent him seeking support for his position on the Treaty from Lee Kuan Yew and Kukrit Pramoj." Mashuri, the Indonesian Information Minister, told Woolcott, that as late as Sunday evening, 22 February, "the situation was 'critical' but that it had been resolved mainly by President Soeharto 'in the Asian [ASEAN?] way through Mushawarah'".

Information on the substantive discussions among the leaders, in particular the "ten eyes" meeting on 24 February, would take time to become known, Woolcott wrote. "Much will probably not filter out, particularly exchanges at casual meetings." Security matters and the political threat North

Vietnam could pose were discussed in the corridors and at the "ten eyes" meeting, but not in detail. East Timor was discussed at the "ten eyes" meeting. "Malaysia and the Philippines were apparently willing to press for a firm statement in support of Indonesia's position. Indonesia did not want this pursued. It wanted to play down the Timor issue which it regards as moving quickly in its direction and does not want to stimulate further avoidable interest in it." Apparently Lee did not raise his doubts about Indonesia's policy, although he explained the reasons for Singapore's abstention at the UN.

Woolcott pointed to some significant points. Obviously the setting-up of the secretariat marked a structural change. Second, while ASEAN had always had a political aspect, "political matters have now been formalized as a major area of ASEAN activity": the declaration called for the harmonization and coordination of views "where desirable". Third, the main emphasis in the public statements was on economic cooperation. The declaration linked security to economic and social development. Fourth, the Heads of Government stated that ASEAN was not a military pact and did not seek to become one, but security cooperation was mentioned. Subversion was stressed as the main threat.

The Heads of Government, fifthly, reiterated their intention to avoid confrontation with the Indo-China states. The declaration called for member states to strive to create conditions conducive to peaceful cooperation among the nations of Southeast Asia on the basis of "mutual respect and mutual benefit", and the treaty of amity was open to other countries in Southeast Asia. The Heads of Government did not, however, reiterate the invitation to the Indo-China states to join ASEAN, though the invitation still stood. Indonesia was not anxious for them to join. Woolcott's initial assessment was that organizationally strengthening ASEAN and enhancing its political role reduced the possibility of close cooperation with the Indo-China states in the near future. It had not, he thought, been very great.

He believed ASEAN would become "more than a consultative club". Problems in the economic area would remain and the Sabah dispute had not been solved. But the summit demonstrated that it had "the ability and the will to surmount important differences". Relations between Singapore and Indonesia had deteriorated before the summit, but Soeharto and Lee had mended their fences. "Indonesian Ministers believe that, when it comes to the crunch, Lee accepts that his own and Singapore's future are to a considerable extent dependent on the success of ASEAN and on his relations with his most immediate and larger neighbours, Indonesia and Malaysia. This limits the degree to which he is, in the end, prepared to press those Singapore interests which conflict with those of Indonesia and Malaysia."

Australia, Woolcott thought, should "move gradually towards developing closer political links with ASEAN, distinct from our bilateral relations with its member states". The Prime Minister (Fraser) had sent a message of greeting, which was read out at the opening, together with similar messages from Canada, Japan, and the EEC.[148] New Zealand had decided against sending one. Had New Zealand been "involved in the affair of the non-invitations", Foreign Affairs officials told the embassy in

Tokyo, "our attitude would perhaps be different". As it was, they thought a message should come later, making some acknowledgment of the summit's significance. "[W]e find it hard to see how a pre-Summit message could avoid some air of affectation and being confined to a general expression of goodwill. Somewhat like a congratulatory telegram to a country wedding, including the wishful thought that all their problems might be little ones." Given the modest expectations ASEAN capitals seemed to have, "we would be diffident about sending a message which anticipated major breakthroughs". Instead the Prime Minister might send separate but identical messages to each leader after the summit.[149] The Acting Minister (Keith Holyoake, as Minister of State) approved that approach.[150]

The Second Summit

In 1977 another summit was held in Kuala Lumpur. This time the JANZ leaders were there. The ASEAN leaders had an informal meeting with the Prime Ministers of Australia, Japan, and New Zealand on 6 August and then separate meetings with the Prime Ministers of each country. "There had been some argument beforehand about the form these meetings should take", the British High Commissioner (Eric Norris) reported. "The Malaysians with their eye over their shoulder at Vietnam were anxious not to make it appear that the eight countries were forming a bloc." They therefore proposed that each Prime Minister should meet the Heads separately. Fraser, however, persuaded the five to sit down with the three for an informal session, though it had "little substance". Pre-summit most attention had been given to Fukuda Takeo. He confirmed Japan's readiness to grant a loan of one billion dollars for the five ASEAN projects when feasibility studies had been completed satisfactorily. ASEAN leaders had hoped to persuade Japan to lower its tariff and non-tariff barriers and make a commitment to a Stabex-type scheme for ASEAN primary commodities. Fukuda, however, "committed himself to very little indeed". ASEAN had also criticized Australia's protectionism. Fraser promised more aid, and Lee and Marcos told him that "though they welcomed the aid they would prefer trade". Muldoon's visit "probably went off best". In his opening speech "he pre-empted any requests by offering greater access to New Zealand markets and increased technical assistance".

The 1977 summit, Norris thought, was "the most important meeting ever held in Malaysia", and the Hilton was like a fortress. But, though there was much ceremony, there was some substance. At the outset Lee had declared "surely we can do better than this" and he did not conceal his disappointment in his closing speech. But the initial scepticism about the summit had been confounded at the opening session when Marcos, "in a well-timed *coup de théâtre*", announced his intention "to take steps to remove the Philippines' claim to Sabah", which had been "a running sore in Malaysian/Philippines relations, and consequently a block on ASEAN progress". At a subsequent press conference, he said he was "working on ways to deal with domestic aspects of the problem (among other things, renunciation may apparently involve amending the Philippines constitution)". But the initial announcement had a positive effect on the summit proceedings. Malaysia would not offer anything in return, lest that suggested the claim had some validity. But Hussein, Marcos, and Soeharto did agree to a Border Crossing and Patrol Agreement.

The closed sessions produced a long "and generally vague" communiqué. The leaders disagreed on the references it should make to Indo-China. Prime Minister Thanin of Thailand wanted a tough line against Indo-Chinese aggression, "physical (against Thailand) and verbal (against ASEAN as a whole)". In the event the references were friendly, expressing a desire for "peaceful and mutually beneficial relations with all countries in the region, including Kampuchea, Laos and Vietnam". Lee argued in vain for a firmer commitment to economic cooperation and intra-ASEAN free trade. It was agreed that the projects should go ahead, "despite differing degrees of enthusiasm and readiness between the five countries. The increasing protectionism in world trade and the need for Stabex arrangements were mentioned, later taken up with the JANZ Prime Ministers. Economic cooperation with the EEC should be intensified, the leaders believed, partly, Norris thought, because of "an apprehension that Japan's expanding economic empire will envelop ASEAN" and "a fear, certainly in Malaysia, that if there is no counterbalance to Japanese involvement ASEAN's options will become severely limited".

The meeting, the High Commissioner concluded, was "a manifestation of political solidarity, even if the economic achievements were thin". Vietnamese criticism and Russian "sniping" were, as Lee said, "a backhanded compliment": if it were "not as solid … as it was, the communist states would not be concerning themselves with the 'threat' which ASEAN presented". ASEAN had indeed become "a sturdier infant" as a result of the summit, Norris concluded, though it was still an infant. "But when one looks back at the disarray which the South-East Asian states were in ten years ago, at ASEAN's inception, and compares that with the situation now, one can see that ASEAN, for all its failings, has contributed to the stability of the region, and has developed the potential to contribute a great deal more. Despite the insistence of some of its members, notably Malaysia, that ASEAN is an economic and cultural association only, its more important positive achievements have so far been in the political and, less openly, in the security fields."[151]

Mervyn Norrish, permanent head of the Ministry of Foreign Affairs in Wellington, thought that ASEAN was "just beginning to add up to more than the sum of its parts". The summit had gone well for New Zealand. "Mr Muldoon's instinct to say all he had to say at once had proved right and the ASEAN delegates agreed with all he said."[152]

Conclusion

The literature on ASEAN is, as it should be, very substantial. It is significant for the fate of states and peoples in Southeast Asia and beyond. It has been both conservative and inventive, developing in ways its creators could not have foreseen, deploying the style and instruments of their diplomacy in novel ways, but without abandoning their essential objective, to limit disputes among themselves and the intervention of states external to the region. This short work can make but a small addition to the literature. But it has suggested that — with the aid indeed of documents drawn from the archives of external powers — it may be possible to study the early years of ASEAN in more detail. That will interest historians, but it may be important to others, too. Words of the great English novelist who called herself George Eliot come to mind.

For want of such real, minute vision of how changes come about in the past, we fall into ridiculously inconsistent estimates of actual movements, condemning in the present what we belaud in the past, and pronouncing impossible processes that have been repeated again and again in the historical preparation of the very system under which we live.[153]

Notes

1. Chandran Jeshurun, *Malaysia: Fifty Years of Diplomacy 1957–2007* (Singapore: Talisman, 2008), p. 75.
2. Cradock/Newsam, 21 Febuary 1958, DO 35/9913 [1], National Archives, Kew.
3. Canadian Embassy Jakarta/Ottawa, 15 January 1959, 33, PM 434/10/1 Pt 2, National Archives, Wellington (hereinafter Pt 2).
4. Reece/Ottawa, 15 January 1959, 28, ibid.
5. Ag Commissioner for New Zealand in South East Asia in Singapore/Wellington, 23 January 1959, ibid.
6. Newton/Ottawa, 23 January 1959, 42, ibid.
7. Preliminary Reactions to Malayan Proposals for Closer Relations between South East Asian Countries, 18 February 1959, ibid.
8. Memorandum, 24 March 1959, ibid.
9. Curwen/Williams, 13 March 1959, DO 35/9913 [34].
10. First Secretary/Wellington, 17 March 1959, Pt 2.
11. Menzies/Ottawa, 18 March 59, 172, ibid.

12. Observations, Malayan Proposals for Closer Economic and Cultural Cooperation in South East Asia, Ibid.
13. Hunt/Smith, 8 May 1959, DO 35/9913 [53].
14. Peren/Wellington, 13 September 1959, Pt 2.
15. Craw/Wellington, 7 August 1959, ibid.
16. Telegram, 18 November 1959, 182S, DO 35/9913 [65].
17. Cradock/Ormerod, 28 December 1959, ibid.
18. Garner/Lloyd, 1 February 1960, 6, FO 371/152140 [D 1022/3], NA, Kew.
19. Crombie/Smith, 3 March 1960, DO 35/9913 [83].
20. Menzies/Ottawa, 7 April 1960, B-31, Pt 2. The China-Burma boundary agreement was concluded in 1960, as was a friendship agreement. Melvin V. Gurtov, *China and Southeast Asia* (Baltimore: Johns Hopkins University Press, 1975), pp. 95–6.
21. Telegram, 28 April 1960, 258, DO 35/9913 [94].
22. Telegram ex Kuala Lumpur, 5 August 1960, 165S, FO 371/152141 [D 1022/30].
23. Minute by ?HLH, 12 September 1960, Pt 2.
24. Note attached to ibid.
25. Telegrams, 14 February 1961, 120, 121, FO 371/159704 [D 1022/8].
26. B.M. Brown for High Commissioner/Wellington, 24 February 1961, Pt. 2.
27. Brown/Wellington, 25 April 1961, Pt 2.
28. Chancery/SEAD, 23 June 1961, FO 371/159704 [D 1022/22].
29. Brown for High Commissioner/Wellington, 30 June 1961, Pt 2. The Thai disappointment over SEATO related to the Western decision to deal with the Laos crisis through a conference at Geneva. See, for example, Peter Busch, *All the Way with LBJ?* (Oxford University Press, 2003), pp. 21–2.
30. Craw/Wellington, 20 July 1961, Pt 2.
31. Arnfinn Jorgensen-Dahl, *Regional Organization in South-East Asia* (New York: St Martin's, 1982), pp. 21–2.
32. Peren for Chargé/Wellington, 11 August 1961, Pt 2.
33. Warner/MacDermot, 23 August 1961, FO 371/159947 [DF 2231/392].

34. Ghazali Shafie, "ASEAN — Today and Tomorrow", *Foreign Affairs Malaysia* 14, no. 4 (December 1981), p. 336.

35. Bennett/Secretary, 28 September 1962, PM 434/10/1.

36. Bennett/Secretary, 9 November 1962, PM 434/10/1.

37. Chapman for High Commissioner/Secretary, 18 April 1963, PM 434/10/1.

38. Quoted in Bernard K. Gordon, *Towards Disengagement in Asia* (Englewood Cliffs: Prentice-Hall, 1969), pp. 104, 102n.

39. Ibid., p. 71. Matthew Jones, *Conflict and Cooperation in South East Asia* (Cambridge: Cambridge University Press, 2002), pp. 195–6.

40. Mackie, p. 318.

41. C.L. Booth Bangkok/Donald Murray SEAD, 17 December 1965, FO 371/180221 [D1121/5].

42. Memo, 6 January 1966, quoted in Gordon, *Towards Disengagement*, p. 117n.

43. Wade/Secretary, 18 March 1966, PM 434/10/1.

44. Weir/Secretary, 13 April 1966, PM 434/10/1.

45. Brief, ANZUS Council meeting, 24 June 1966, PM 434/10/1.

46. Hunn for High Commissioner/Secretary, 1 July 1966, PM 434/10/1.

47. Telegram ex Rumbold, 3 June 1966, 410, FO 371/185931 [D1121/15].

48. Phillips/Murray, 16 August 1966, FO 371/185931 [D1121/31].

49. Quoted in M. Leifer, *Indonesia's Foreign Policy* (London: Allen and Unwin, 1983), p. 115.

50. Phillips/Murray, 30 January 1967, FCO 24/16[5], National Archives, London.

51. Phillips/Murray, 30 January 1967, FCO 24/16 [6].

52. Enclosure A in Bentley/Mason, 7 February 1967, FCO 24/16[4].

53. Wade/Secretary, 10 March 1967, PM 434/10/1.

54. Telegram, 28 February 1967, 6S, FCO 24/16[16].

55. Edmonds/Secretary, 3 March 1967, PM 434/10/1.

56. Commissioner/Secretary, 14 March 1967, PM 434/10/1.

57. Addis/Murray, 10 March 1967, FCO 24/16 [21].

58. Quoted in Jorgensen-Dahl, p. 33.

59. Telegram, 22 May 1967, 496, FCO 24/16[40].
60. Roger Irvine, "The Formative Years of ASEAN: 1967–1975", in *Understanding ASEAN* edited by A. Broinowski (New York: St Martin's, 1982), p. 13.
61. Zohrab/Secretary, 15 August 1967, PM 434/12/1.
62. Weir/Secreary, 24 August 1967, PM 434/12/1.
63. Commissioner/Secretary, 18 August 1967, PM 434/12/1.
64. Irvine, p. 14.
65. Aust DEA/all posts, 5 September 1967, PM 434/12/1.
66. Laking/all posts, Regional Cooperation in South East Asia, 6 November 1967, PM 434/12/1.
67. Ooi Kee Beng, *The Reluctant Politician* (Singapore: Institute of Southeast Asian Studies, 2006), pp. 168–9.
68. Quoted in H. Heiner, *ASEAN and the ZOPFAN Concept* (Singapore: Institute of Southeast Asian Studies, 1991), p. 13.
69. Quoted in Noordin Sopiee, "The 'Neutralisation' of South-East Asia", in *Asia and the Western Pacific*, edited by Hedley Bull (Melbourne: Nelson, 1975), pp. 137–8.
70. Quoted in Dick Wilson, *The Neutralization of Southeast Asia* (New York, Washington: Praeger, 1975), p. 43.
71. "The Neutralisation of Southeast Asia", *Pacific Community* 3, no. 1 (October 1971), pp. 110–17.
72. Ibid., pp. 115–16.
73. Hanggi, pp. 59–60.
74. Memo, High Commissioner/Wellington, 10 December 1971, PM 343/12/1 Pt 2, National Archives, Wellington.
75. Telegram ex Singapore, 18 April 1972, 217, ibid.
76. Memo, H.H. Francis/Wellington, 26 April 1972, ibid.
77. Memo, Chargé/Wellington, 18 May 1972, ibid.
78. Memo, 22 May 1972, ibid.
79. Memo, N.Haffey/Ottawa, 26 June 1972, 148, ibid., Pt 3.
80. Middleton/Chick, 18 July 1972, FCO 24/1270[32].
81. Telegram ex Australian Embassy, Manila, 17 July 1972, 1164, PM 343/12/1 Pt 3.
82. Telegram, 20 July 1972, 2169, ibid.

83. Middlebrook/Slatcher, 30 January 1973, FCO 24/1529 [13]
84. Telegram, 21 February 1973, 182, Pt 3.
85. Telegram, 2 March 1973, 330, 434/12/1 Pt 4.
86. Telegram, 13 April 1973, 364, Ibid.
87. Telegram, 21 April 1973, 387, PM 343/12/1 Pt 4.
88. Tony Ford/Chick, 14 August 1973, FCO 24/1530 [50].
89. Regionalism and Neutralisation, Notes for Opening Remarks, 15 October 1973?, FCO 24/1530[59].
90. Warner/Butler, 12 April 1961, and enclosure, FO 371/159835 [DF 1015/477], National Archives, Kew.
91. Australia Telegram, 10 May 1974, 1965, PM 434/12/1 Pt 5.
92. M. Stuart-Fox, *Buddhist Kingdom Marxist State* (Bangkok: White Lotus, 1996), pp. 56–7.
93. Simcock/SyFA, 20 May 1974, Pt 5.
94. Telegram, 31 May 1974, 542, ibid.
95. Submission to PM, 28 January 1974, Pt 4.
96. Telegram, 14 February 1974, 164, ibid.
97. Memo, Ambassador/Secretary, 19 March 1974.
98. Telegram to Kuala Lumpur, 27 August 1974, 982 Pt 5.
99. Telegram ex Singapore, 6 September 1974, 838, ibid.
100. Telegram ex Richards, Hong Kong, 23 October 1974, 509, ibid.
101. Telegram ex Kuala Lumpur, 30 October 1974, 1310, ibid.
102. Telegram ex Singapore, 12 November 1974, 1038, Pt 5.
103. To all posts, 11 November 1974, Pt 5.
104. Irvine, p. 32.
105. Quoted in Irvine, p 32.
106. Quoted in Irvine, p. 32.
107. *Financial Times*, 14 May 1975.
108. *Times*, 14 May 1975.
109. Irvine, p. 35.
110. ibid.
111. Jorgensen-Dahl, p. 84. Tunku Abdul Rahman Putra, *Looking Back* (Kuala Lumpur: Pustaka Antara, 1977), p. 161.
112. Jorgensen-Dahl, p. 84.

113. David Irvine, "Making Haste Less Slowly: ASEAN from 1975", in *Understanding ASEAN* edited by Broinowski, p. 42.

114. New Zealand telegram ex Kuala Lumpur, 15 January 1976, 41, FCO 15/2173.

115. A.C. Stuart Jakarta/Murray Simons SEAD, 9 February 1976, FCO/2173 [8].

116. Australian telegram ex Bangkok, 11 February 1976, 8329, Pt 7.

117. Australian telegram, 13 February 1976, 7609, FCO 15/2173 [13].

118. Australian telegram ex Singapore, 13 February 1976, 7608, FCO 15/2173 [13]. The references to Malaysia and Brunei presumably relate to the challenges the former was delivering to the protectorate status of the latter. Andrew T.H. Tan, *Security Perspectives of the Malay Archipelago* (Cheltenham: Elgar, 2004), p. 93.

119. Australian telegram ex Kuala Lumpur, 13 February 1976, 7573, FCO 15/2173. Once his supporter, the federal government found Mustapha's attitude too autonomous.

120. J.L. Brooke Bkk/R.P. Barston SEAD, 18 February 1976, FCO 15/2173 [11].

121. New Zealand telegram ex Tokyo, 4 February 1966, 108, Part 7.

122. New Zealand telegram ex Kuala Lumpur, 5 February 1976, 137, Pt 7.

123. Stuart/Simons, 9.2. as above.

124. New Zealand telegram ex Bangkok, 11 February 1976, 118, Pt 7.

125. Australian telegram, 14 February 1976, 7608 as above. Vietnam did indeed see ASEAN as a "new SEATO". Allan Gyngell, "Looking outwards", in *Understanding ASEAN* edited by Broinowski, p. 129.

126. Telegram to Singapore, 3 February 1976, 148, Pt. 7

127. Telegram to Tokyo, 9 February 1976, 115, Pt 7.

128. Brooke/Barston, 18 February 1976, 115, Pt 7.

129. New Zealand telegram ex Singapore, 17 February 1976, 196, Pt 7.

130. New Zealand telegram ex Singapore, 18 February 1976, 201, Pt 7.

131. New Zealand telegram ex Jakarta, 18 February 1976, 141, Pt 7

132. Australian telegram, 18 February 1976, 7622, Pt 7.

133. New Zealand telegram ex Kuala Lumpur, 19 February 1976, 199, Pt. 7.
134. Stuart/Simons, 23 February 1976, FCO 15/2173 [15]
135. Copy in Hanggi, pp. 65–8.
136. D. Irvine, p. 49.
137. M.L. Suriyamongkol, "The Politics of Economic Cooperation in the Association of South East Asian Nations" (PhD dissertation, University of Illinois at Urbana-Champaign, 1982), p. 195.
138. New Zealand telegram ex Singapore, 24 February 1976, 225, Pt 7.
139. Ford/Callaghan, 1 March 1976, despatch 022/1, FCO 15/2174 [34].
140. Australian telegram, 26 February 1976, 7717, Pt. 7.
141. Canadian telegram, 27 February 1976, 403, Pt 7.
142. Memo, 1 March 1976, FCO 15/2173 [24].
143. Memo, 3 March 1976, FCO 15/2173 [27].
144. Ricketts/Jones, 8 March 1976, FCO 15/2174 [43].
145. Peter Tripp/H.A.H. Cortazzi, 8 March 1976, FCO15/2174 [44].
146. Australian telegram ex Kuala Lumpur, March 1976, 8147, FCO 15/2174 [45].
147. Enclosure in Colin Munro for T.H. Gee/Jones, 15 March 1976, FCO 15/2174 [47].
148. Woolcott/Peacock, 3 March 1976, FCO 15/2174 [56].
149. New Zealand telegram to Tokyo, February 1976, 179. Pt 7.
150. Memo by Norrish, 23 February 1976, initialled KJH, 25 February 1976, Pt. 7.
151. High Commissioner/Secretary of State, 15 August 1977, confidential, FCO 24/2340 [33].
152. Conversation at British High Commission, Wellington, 28 November 1977, FCO 24/2340 [34].
153. Quoted in Ruth A. Solie, *Music in Other Words* (Berkeley, Los Angeles, 2004), p. 158.

Index

About the Author

Nicholas Tarling is a retired Professor of History from the University of Auckland, where he was also Dean of the Faculty of Arts, Chairman of the Deans Committee, and Deputy Vice-Chancellor. He was the founder and president of the New Zealand Asian Studies Society (NZASIA). In retirement he has been a Fellow of the New Zealand Asia Institute and has served as Director of the Institute and later of the International Office.

His books on Asian history include *Britain, the Brookes and Brunei* (1971), *Sulu and Sabah* (1978), *The Burthen, the Risk and the Glory* (1982), and *The Fourth Anglo-Burman War* (1987). He also edited the *Cambridge History of Southeast Asia*. In retirement he has completed a trilogy on British policy in Southeast Asia during the Pacific War, the Cold War and the Korean War, a book on the Japanese interregnum, *A Sudden Rampage*, and a trilogy on imperialism, nationalism and regionalism in Southeast Asia.